More Innovative Games

Brenda Lichtman, PhD

Sam Houston State University

Human Kinetics

Library of Congress Cataloging-in-Publication Data

Lichtman, Brenda, 1948-
More innovative games / by Brenda Lichtman.
p. cm.
Includes bibliographical references and index.
ISBN 0-88011-712-5
1. Physical education for children. 2. Games. I. Title.
GV443.L516 1999
372.86--dc21 98-39169
CIP

ISBN: 0-88011-712-5

Acquisitions Editor: Scott Wikgren; **Developmental Editor**: Laura Casey Mast; **Assistant Editors**: Cynthia McEntire, Jennifer Goldberg, Laurie Stokoe; **Copyeditor**: Donald Amerman; **Proofreader**: Sarah Wiseman; **Indexer**: L. Pilar Wyman; **Graphic Designer**: Robert Reuther; **Graphic Artist**: Sandra Meier; **Cover Designer**: Jack Davis; **Illustrators**: Roberto Sabas, Tom Roberts; **Printer**: United Graphics

Printed in the United States of America

10 9 8 7 6 5 4 3 2 1

Human Kinetics
Web site: http://www.humankinetics.com/

United States: Human Kinetics
P.O. Box 5076, Champaign, IL 61825-5076
1-800-747-4457
e-mail: humank@hkusa.com

Canada: Human Kinetics
475 Devonshire Road Unit 100, Windsor, ON N8Y 2L5
1-800-465-7301 (in Canada only)
e-mail: humank@hkcanada.com

Europe: Human Kinetics
P.O. Box IW14, Leeds LS16 6TR, United Kingdom
(44) 1132 781708
e-mail: humank@hkeurope.com

Australia: Human Kinetics
57A Price Avenue, Lower Mitcham, South Australia 5062
(088) 277 1555
e-mail: humank@hkaustralia.com

New Zealand: Human Kinetics
P.O. Box 105-231, Auckland 1
(09) 523 3462
e-mail: humank@hknewz.com

To my parents,
who encouraged me to explore,
provided me with opportunities to experience,
and allowed me the freedom to create.

Purple leaves do grow on trees,
if you allow yourself to see them.

Contents

PREFACE ix

ACKNOWLEDGMENTS xi

Chapter 1 **Encouraging Creativity** 1

Unlocking Creativity, Discovering Innovation 2
Creativity: An Elusive Term 3
The Professional's Role 4
Where Do You Start? 7
The Additive Approach to Game Creation 10
Organize an Intramural, Field-Day Experience, or Olympic Extravaganza 11

Chapter 2 **Evolution of an Innovative Game: A Student's Work in Progress** 13

The Most Often Asked Questions 14
The Nurturing Process From Inception to the Final Product 18
Subsequent Changes 23

Chapter 3 **Developing Hybrid Activities** 25

The Games 26
Soccer Croquet—Four Ways 26
Dodge Basketball 31
Flag Basketball 35
Soccer Flag Football 38
Multi-Option Ball 40

Chapter 4 **Creating Excitement With Nontraditional Equipment** 45

The Games 46
Bottlecap Golf 47
Volley-Tennis Broom Ball 50
Sheetball Brigade 54

Towel Ball Pin Bombardment ... *58*
Milk Jug Football ... *61*

Chapter 5 Discovering New Possibilities Through Altered Actions ... 65

The Games ... 66
Scooter Slalom ... *66*
Scooterized Volleyball ... *72*
Beachball Locomotion ... *74*
Limb Bombardment ... *77*
Three-Armed Basketball ... *79*

Chapter 6 Modifying Goals and Player Setup ... 83

The Games ... 84
Running Bases ... *84*
Basket Hoop Bombardment ... *87*
Dot Baseball and Box Baseball ... *89*
Soft-Volleyball ... *93*
Tennis Backboard Basketball ... *95*
Punchball in the Round ... *97*
Team Tennis-Volley ... *100*
Frontline Shift Volleyball ... *102*

Chapter 7 Finding New Uses for Standard Equipment ... 107

The Games ... 108
Frisbee Soccer ... *108*
Cone Slide Bombardment ... *111*
Endline Ball ... *113*
Frisbee Skeet Bowling ... *116*
Hand-Minton and Milk Jug-Minton ... *119*

Chapter 8 Providing Multimedia Adaptations ... 123

Television ... 123
Video and Pinball Games ... 124
Recreational Board Games ... 124
The Games ... 125
Tic-Tac-Toe Multiple Ways ... *125*
Battleship ... *129*
Pole Foosball ... *132*
Action Clue ... *136*
Roller Trash Can Basketball ... *141*

Chapter 9 Utilizing Unique Locales and Underused Spaces 147

The Games 148
Rebound Bowling *148*
Hallball Three Ways *152*
One-Walled Volleyball *156*
Corner Ball *159*

Chapter 10 Developing Multi-Principled Creations 161

The Games 163
Ricochet Fungo Softball *163*
Soft-Volley-Soccer *168*
Foosball Kaleidoscope *171*
Basket-Mazeball *175*

REFERENCES AND SUGGESTED SOURCES 181
INDEX 183
ABOUT THE AUTHOR 187

Preface

In the world of physical activities, novelty and freshness last only as long as overexposure can be avoided. *Innovative Games* (Lichtman 1993) provided more than 35 games that served to insulate offerings from the "oh, that again" syndrome (an infectious malady common in programs that rely too heavily on the triad of volleyball, basketball, and softball). Since so many curricula rehash activities that students have experienced year after year, it is no wonder that boredom results. Without constant expansion and development of games, the luster of what was considered new and innovative begins to fade, again leaving physical educators and recreational professionals faced with the challenge of finding different ways to achieve our objectives, yet keep motivation high. The solution to this dilemma can be found in *More Innovative Games*. Building on the success of the first book, you will find an additional four to seven games illustrating each of the six original principles: Developing Hybrid Activities, Creating Excitement With Nontraditional Equipment, Discovering New Possibilities Through Altered Actions, Modifying Goals and Player Setup, Finding New Uses for Standard Equipment, and Providing Multimedia Adaptations. Furthermore, two new tenets have been added: Utilizing Unique Locales and Underused Spaces, and Developing Multi-Principled Creations.

While each volume can stand independently, together they reinforce each other, providing even greater insurance against program stagnation. By understanding and applying one or a combination of these principles, you—and even your students—will be able to devise your own innovative activities. To aid you in your endeavor, chapter 2 provides a step-by-step description of the processes required to take an idea and, through application of appropriate feedback, have students modify their initial concept into a well-conceived, innovative activity. By following this procedure, you can foster your participants' interests and reward them with the mechanisms underlying divergent thinking and the devising of novel ideas.

In *More Innovative Games* you will find more than 40 games that can be integrated immediately into programs for children in grades 6 through 12. Any equipment not readily available can be solicited from local merchants, purchased at garage sales, or collected from participants' families.

Equipment needs are listed for the number of active participants in each game.

The activities are organized in a consistent easy-to-follow format. After a brief overview, the "Objectives" section identifies the goals that each activity seeks to develop, ensures accountability, and helps curriculum planners understand where best to integrate the game into the existing program.

"Helpful Hints" offers variations along with alterations to make games less difficult or more challenging, depending on the needs of the participants. For those who provide instruction for upper elementary aged children, an "Adaptations for Younger Participants" section is included for many of the games. However, some activities can be incorporated without modification for younger children. Where multiple variations of the same activity can be applied, these are described, along with any alteration of rules and regulations, within the context of the initial description of the game.

"Playing Area" indicates the type of facility best suited for the activity. In about one quarter of the games, large numbers of participants can be accommodated in a relatively small space. "Participants" specifies the number of active players, and where applicable, identifies their positions or roles. Additionally, since a number of games require novel motor patterns, or ones rarely used, some neutralization of skill discrepancy among participants results. Also listed is the number of officials needed for the activity to progress smoothly, and where their responsibilities might not be obvious, their roles and positioning are specified.

The "Game" description provides you with the most pertinent details for successfully introducing the activity. Any exceptions to rules that carry over from well-known activities are noted, and any stipulations regarding concerns for safety are reinforced. For most team activities, you can easily draw from your own experiences and apply them, but if an innovative activity does not have a traditional model, its specifics are explained in detail.

Competitive activities can result in injury, regardless of the degree to which you exercise prudent restraint. Unique "Safety Considerations" are addressed, but as a professional you must ensure that general safety precautions are followed.

The requirements for the activities in *More Innovative Games* are not etched in stone. Unlike traditional games, these don't have years of exposure that have honed them to a precise form. Use the activities in whatever ways are best for your situation. In doing so, perhaps you'll never again hear a student say, "Oh, that again."

Acknowledgments

Without eager, captive audiences serving as guinea pigs, I would have had few opportunities to try, modify, and, in some instances, totally overhaul my creations. The undergraduate and graduate students at Sam Houston State University have served effectively in this vital capacity. In doing so, they have been a constant source of inspiration and encouragement. The feedback from these patient and astute critics has been invaluable, and their exuberance extremely heartwarming. In each class, as they inspect the variety of equipment, they are like kids in a candy store, restless to know what the day's activities will bring. After an hour or more of non-stop innovative activities, even though they are hot, sweaty, and rather tired, many want a preview of the games that will be on tap for the next session. This enthusiasm gives me a never-ending source of encouragement. So, to these students I give thanks.

Encouraging Creativity

When was the last time your students came to you brimming with enthusiasm, asking, "What are we going to play today?" If you're like most physical education and recreation instructors, you can't remember such an instance.

We could make a difference in disinterested attitudes by expanding our usual yearly program evaluations and looking at our curricular offerings from the participants' points of view. We may see our curricula as varied, when in fact we present the same activities year after year. In large part, the content of our learning units is very similar across grades 6 to 12: rewarming skills, revisiting standard strategies, and rehashing rules. This conflagration is fueled because many of the same activities are offered in community-based recreation leagues, intramural programs, and interscholastic sports. Viewed in this light, is it surprising that many teenagers perceive organized activity programs as the same old stuff?

Our activity programs must compete with the dozens of entertainment choices young people have at their fingertips. If choice and variety are part of the key to keeping adolescents' interest high, our curricular offerings must diversify to avoid what I call the "oh, that again" syndrome, which produces a seeming lack of motivation in participants. The cure lies in the periodic infusion of novel activities. Although such additions are not a panacea, they can help break the standard repetitive cycle, while providing variety and a sense of freshness to program offerings.

Does this mean that we should abandon the traditional activities of basketball, volleyball, softball, and the like? Absolutely not, for these sports provide valuable skills and knowledge and help to shape desirable affective behaviors. If we hope to instill in our participants a love of movement that they will carry throughout their lives, we need to spice up our programs, making them more innovative and less predictable. At the same time, we can meet our overall goals and objectives.

Unlocking Creativity, Discovering Innovation

Many theorists have struggled to devise a clear and concise definition of creativity (Adams, 1986; Haefele, 1962; Mooney & Razik, 1967; Ochse, 1990; Parnes & Harding, 1962; Shank, 1988; Steinberg, 1988). They imply that the creative person has an ability to think in a divergent manner and a skill for integrating information in a unique way that produces a fresh approach. For many experts, innovation is the key ingredient in creativity. Most people believe that creativity is desirable, yet as Ralph Waldo Emerson pointed out in "The American Scholar" in 1837 (Porte, 1983, pp. 58–59), schools and colleges in the 19th century often did little to foster its development, drilling students rather than requiring them to synthesize and integrate facts.

Even after 150 years of supposed progress within our schools, Silberman (1970), Holt (1974), Sarason (1990), Schlechty (1990), and Toch (1991) claimed not much has changed. Schools barely tolerate divergent behavior and thinking through the early elementary grades, and they offer little positive reinforcement for its continuation. Rather, we teach children in both subtle and direct ways that conformity is more desirable. When the child who uses a blue crayon to draw a tree trunk is reminded that trees are brown, or when the person who questions why the rules in badminton and tennis are different is told, "That's just the way those sports are played," we are sending the message that we reward thinking that meshes with the norm. In the process, we are destroying our children's curiosity and their desire to think or act independently.

This problem extends beyond everyday program decision making to the makeup of the entire curriculum. We are reluctant to allow students greater responsibility in making decisions about content. Yet, as Bok (1986) points out in *Higher Learning:*

> *More and more, the United States will have to live by its wits, prospering or declining according to the capacity of its people to develop new ideas, to work with sophisticated technology, to create new products and imaginative new ways of solving problems. Of all our national assets, a trained intelligence and a capacity for innovation and discovery seem destined to be the most important. (jacket cover)*

The world is besieged with enormously difficult issues (crime, drug abuse, ecological concerns, a limited health-care system, and economic problems) that will need to be confronted in novel ways because standard solutions no longer work.

Tye and Novotney (1975) were sensitive to this issue when they wrote that,

> *for the educator, the problem is clear: how can the children of today be educated to live in the world that hardly can be imagined but which will be upon us with appalling rapidity? Clearly, our traditional approach to schooling will not be adequate to handle the task, and we must begin now to restructure our educational system. The question is, what implications do these projections of the future hold for schools and in which directions should today's educators begin their planning (p. 19)?*

As professionals, we must change our focus to emphasize innovative approaches that provide plausible solutions and offer unique possibilities.

Creativity: An Elusive Term

We use the term *creativity* without a second thought, but a precise description is difficult to pin down. Reber's (1985) approach seems most workable. She considers creativity "a mental process that leads to solutions, ideas, conceptualizations, artistic forms, theories or products that are unique and novel" (p. 28). This process involves the ability to generalize relationships and to bridge conceptual gaps, and it ultimately leads to creation, which in turn results in something useful that did not exist before. The inventor devises new products after careful choices rather than by some rote or iterative process.

Creativity depends upon motive and opportunity. Research suggests that besides taking risks and having spontaneity, independence, self-confidence, liveliness, impulsiveness, and high tolerance of ambiguity, creative individuals are intrinsically motivated. They gain satisfaction from engaging in the creative process, which serves as an end in itself. Although they take pleasure in the result, the product or tangible reward is not their driving force (Haefele, 1962; Shank, 1988; Steinberg, 1988). If you encourage adolescents to devise novel games, you help them look at problems in alternative ways, a major component of creativity, while they also get the chance to enjoy the fruits of their labor.

The Professional's Role

Do you encourage a "coloring book" approach to thinking? Preset outlines strangle creativity by requiring a person to stay within the fixed lines. We need to provide an atmosphere in which individuals are willing to attempt to develop new games. At the same time, we must keep in mind that the games don't have to be perfect to possess intrinsic value. Those whom we lead and teach are not on a mission to invent the next sport to be adopted by the Olympics. Our goal is to have participants devise activities that differ from the standard fare to which they have been exposed. By following the simple guidelines in figure 1.1, we can help adolescents achieve this objective.

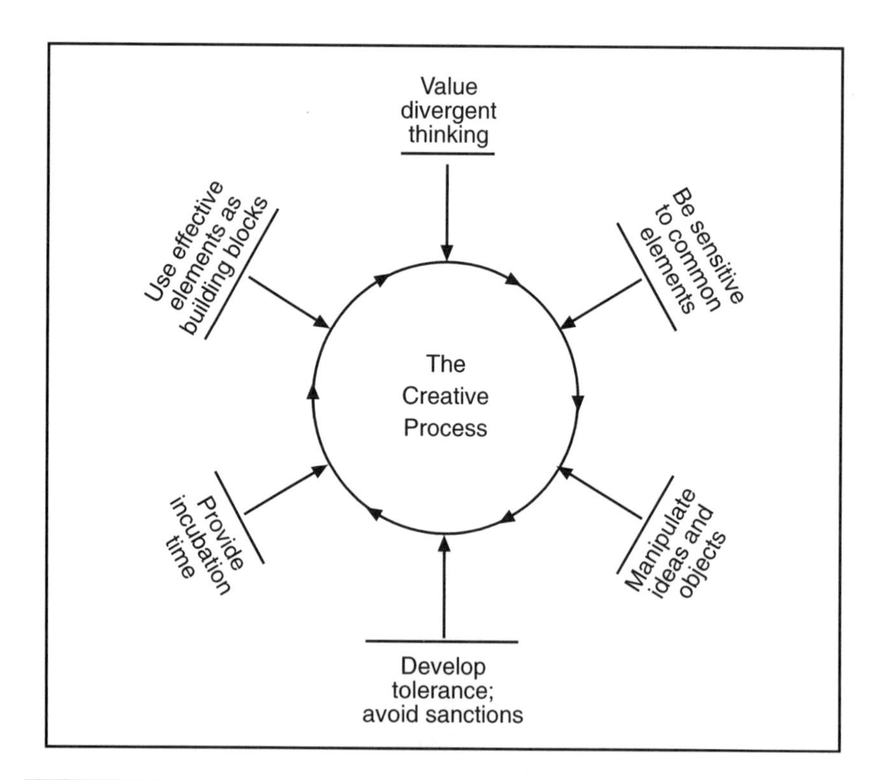

Figure 1.1 Guidelines for encouraging creativity.
Reprinted, by permission, from Lichtman, B., 1993, *Innovative Games* (Champaign, IL: Human Kinetics), 4.

Value Divergent Thinking

Unless you place a premium on developing innovative games, participants are not likely to spend the time and effort required for this creative endeavor. By encouraging exploration of different approaches to accomplishing a specific objective, you provide an open environment in which experimentation is valued. Setting an example by devising your own new activities, or at least selecting and implementing games students have not played before, is essential. By doing this you'll reinforce their desire and pique their curiosity to experience different activities.

Be Sensitive to Common Elements

Make participants more sensitive to their environment and the common elements that comprise a game to promote creativity. Obviously, every game must possess a goal or objective, but if you define it precisely from the start, you stifle, rather than enhance, the creative process. Imagine trying to think in global terms if the stated goal was that "players try to score points by kicking a soccer ball through the uprights of a football goal post." You would focus on soccer. By substituting the objective of propelling a ball into an area defined as a target or goal, you open up limitless possibilities. Once the goal is identified, a series of questions like those in table 1.1 can be posed that will serve to determine the major elements of the activity.

Manipulate Ideas and Objects

Identifying the activity's strengths and shortcomings is the next step. Your group's analysis should be balanced; if you pay attention to only the negative aspects and ignore positive features, you risk curing a problem while detracting from a desirable feature. You should devise and test more than one solution for a problem and choose the most effective one. After you eliminate the major pitfalls, address some of the less critical factors. Finally, fine-tune the game by playing it.

Develop Tolerance and Avoid Sanctions

Novel activities often require unique rules, player setups, court design, and so on. It may be inappropriate to use preexisting patterns from traditional sports or even other innovative games. Yet at the same time, you don't need to reinvent the whole wheel each time you create a new activity. If you reward students for adopting a what-if attitude and reinforce it with your let's-try-it approach, you will send a clear message that using elements that seem to have worked in similar situations is fine, but allowing imaginations to devise unique, but workable, solutions is also valued.

Table 1.1

Factors to Consider During the Games Creation Process

Major element	Questions
Goal	What is the general objective? What method(s) exist for scoring?
Equipment	What items? How many? Any special requirements? Other materials and supplies?
Playing area	What facilities? Are these critical? Does selection impact the equipment to be used? Facility size and layout? Special markings and their functions? Where are goals to be positioned?
Participants	Is there a minimum, maximum, or ideal number? What are the player positions and their responsibilities? Do players assume a specific configuration? Are other people needed, such as scorers or referees?
Game	What method(s) of locomotion? Are there any special requirements? What rules are needed? What is required in the general flow of the activity? How is success or winning determined?
Safety concerns	Are there any special safety considerations? Can the game be made safer by altering the rules, changing the equipment, changing court setup, and so on? If changes are made, how will they impact the game?

Often people misinterpret constructive criticism, believing that criticism is directed at them personally, rather than at an idea. To encourage an open dialogue, you must make it clear that eliminating a particular aspect of an activity does not mean that the person who suggested it is stupid, for the same idea might be perfect in a different activity setting. It is extremely important to realize that there is no absolute formula to apply to the process of creation or to the modification of original ideas. Rather, it takes a good dose of educated guesswork to smooth out the glitches.

Provide Incubation Time

Time is a critical factor in the creative process. Ideas need to simmer to some degree before they can be translated into a workable form. Small group discussion is an ideal way to plant the seeds that grow to novel ideas, but without time for personal introspection and consideration, end products may not be as rich or as well thought out as possible. Reluctance to sacrifice activity time for group interchange is understandable, but sharing is essential for the developmental process to proceed.

Perhaps you could devote part of a rainy day or study hall to this task. When a lesson or practice calls for station work, consider including a "think tank" station where the elements of a novel activity can be devised or fine-tuned. In school settings, homework could be assigned or informal interchange could be encouraged in locker rooms, in transit to playing fields, and during lunch periods.

Use Effective Elements as Building Blocks

Football and baseball undergo rule changes almost annually. Naismith's version of basketball was a far cry from the game we know today. In other words, games undergo continual evolution. But new developments aren't necessarily good ones. What do you do if, after careful consideration and even a consensus among group members, some suggestions or even entire games just don't seem to work?

First, don't automatically throw the baby out with the bath water. Elements can surely be salvaged and used as the nucleus for devising an alternative that does function successfully. Second, something you're tempted to judge a dismal failure need not be viewed in such absolute terms. There is inherent value in engaging adolescents in the constructive process of thinking and devising unique alternatives to standard curriculum offerings that will impact their physical education and recreational experiences. By doing so, you change the psychological emphasis in the gymnasium setting from passive to active cognitive processing. Success in creating a new game is not defined merely in terms of the utilitarian function of the product, but in the effort and motivation expended to push back the barriers that all too often confine our thinking. It is this pushing back and opening up that helps us define ourselves by making us aware of what we are capable of accomplishing and allows us as individuals the freedom to explore and expand our thinking.

Where Do You Start?

There may be psychological safety in continuing with "the same old stuff," but the SOS approach spells danger. It erects a barrier against change, and the fear of failure prevents us from becoming risk-takers. Nothing awful will come if you are wrong or if things don't go as smoothly as planned. Isn't it better to try and fail than to do nothing? Help provide participants the motivation they need to begin by introducing games they haven't experienced, offering them the opportunity to engage in the creative process, and encouraging and recognizing their efforts.

Broaden Experiences

Your first step will be to broaden the activities in your curriculum or program. This should enhance learners' interest and provide meaning and value. Start by introducing a few of the games described in chapters 3 through 10. These include

- developing hybrid activities by melding elements from two or more standard sports or games;
- using nontraditional equipment such as trash cans, plastic half-gallon jugs, and the like as an integral part of a game;
- altering locomotion and manipulation;
- modifying the goal of a typical activity or using a unique player setup;
- finding new uses for standard equipment;
- creating activities by adapting ideas from multimedia presentations (television, films, videos, arcade and board games, etc.);
- adapting or creating activities to be played in seldom- or underutilized spaces (hallways, outside concrete or brick walls, stairwells, etc.); and
- melding different principles together, or amalgamating existing innovative activities that draw from two or more of these seven tenets.

One of these principles, multimedia adaptations, provides an excellent place to begin. The typical American watches television for close to four hours per day (Dietz & Gortmaker, 1985), and game shows such as "Wheel of Fortune," "Jeopardy," and "American Gladiators" are especially popular. You can capitalize on some of the interest in these games by incorporating elements from them in your program. Basic requirements of some of the challenges posed on "American Gladiators," for example, can be lifted and modified to gentler and more appropriate forms. The event in which a contestant is required to swing on a set of rings to a goal area without being knocked off the suspended rings is simply a form of tag using a novel means of locomotion. Couldn't you create an alternative using innovative locomotor patterns that aren't as hazardous? Another "American Gladiators" challenge requires the contestant to hit a target before being hit himself. Doesn't that seem very much like high-tech bombardment? What if players aimed at inanimate objects? You can modify the goal to make it age appropriate and safe, while keeping the excitement of the game.

Create a Video

As a student being asked to create a novel activity, imagine how you would feel watching the creations of others who came before you in that program, especially if some of the participants were peers whom you could recognize. Reactions such as "Wow, that looks like fun," and "When can we play that?" are bound to emerge and in the process spark an enthusiasm for getting involved. You might not possess the technical skills to create the video, but many schools have programs where students, under the guidance of a trained faculty member, learn the required processes. Such a situation provides opportunities for collaborative efforts, helping students to realize the integrative value of much of what transpires in courses. If more than one school or school district is participating in such a project, videos can be exchanged, increasing the number and variety of novel games, not to mention broader applications at the state and national levels.

Create a Games Book

One useful project is to devise a games book of the activities participants develop. Future groups can play the games, which will also serve as models for creations by other classes. Having models is critical, for initially teenagers will reflect society's pervasive attitudes: "If it's not broken, don't fix it" and "It probably won't work or someone would have thought of it before." These ideas filter down from the highest administrative levels to our clientele. The games book can convince others that devising novel activities is not reserved only for those who possess special gifts. When adolescents realize that their peers played an integral role in developing a novel activity you introduced to them, they seem to shed their negative mindset for a more positive, receptive, and self-assured attitude. This book should be accessible, and found in various locales throughout the school or organization. Consider these possibilities for placement: library, administrative offices, physical educators' or recreational specialists' offices, bulletin boards, and cases in which notable items are displayed for the public's consumption.

Direct Small-Group Brainstorming

Once a few shows or videos have been identified as the building blocks upon which innovative games can be developed, divide into small groups of four to five people each. You can assign a program or video game or let each group choose one to use as the springboard for its own game. If restrictions must be applied (for example, if the game has to be played in a given facility or a minimum number of participants must be accommodated), establish them at the very beginning. Let the brainstorming proceed for 5 to 10 minutes. The goal at this point is to identify the basic elements of the new activity, not to refine them. Provide incubation time by assigning participants to think about the ideas that were discussed within the group. At the next opportunity, have group members exchange their thoughts and settle on one avenue to pursue in greater detail.

Once the major elements have been identified, the group should present the outline of the activity to you, the instructor. You should scrutinize the game for any obvious safety hazards and offer feedback about them but avoid suggesting solutions. Instead, ask the group to arrive at viable alternatives. Do not point out other weaknesses. While it is tempting and perhaps expedient to do so, it will defeat part of your purpose. Once the safety issues are resolved, allow the group no more than 5 to 10 minutes to try out its creation. Glaring shortcomings will become obvious to the students.

At the third meeting, let the group modify the activity to rectify the problems found in their game, or at least reduce them to a tolerable level. Provide additional opportunities for small-group participation to determine if the suggestions were successful in ameliorating the major problems.

Once the group has reached this point, usually at a fourth meeting, it is time to describe and demonstrate the activity to the other groups. In order to ensure clarity of abstract concepts, unless the group includes an older high school student, you may want to explain the activity yourself rather than give that responsibility to a group member. Again, 5 to 10 minutes of play are adequate and will allow participants to ask questions and provide additional feedback. This feedback is the foundation for further modifications. The process of implementing suggestions and analyzing their consequences will, in most cases, alter the activity to produce a viable program option.

The Additive Approach to Game Creation

Another technique to use in a small-group setting is an additive method for developing a novel activity. In this approach, each person in a group defines one element in the innovative activity. These elements might include playing area, equipment, object of the game, number of players, players' general responsibilities and positions, and the type of locomotor patterns permitted.

So, in the additive approach, the first person might decide that the game is to take place on a soccer field, and the second elects to use baseball bats, Wiffle balls, and trash cans. The third individual decides how this equipment could be used in that setting; one alternative would be to hit whiffle balls fungo-style into the trash cans. The fourth person would determine the flow of this activity by deciding whether it would be a cooperative effort or a competitive game for two teams. In the case of competition, members of both teams could hit balls over the midfield line to their team's designated trash can targets. Shaggers could return those balls that did not score a goal. If the entire group worked together over a set period of time to improve upon the best previous score, cooperation would be the major focus, instead of competition.

Once the basic plan for the activity is devised, participants will need to experiment with the actions to determine reasonable distances, how much equipment will be required, and what rules must be implemented so the game can progress smoothly and effectively. While refinement of the game is taking place, you should stress safety factors. In the game just described, the activity changes the usual goal of batting, which typically does not require participants to project an object into a receptacle. Occasionally, use of this progressive developmental approach will result in an activity that integrates two or more principles rather than using only one. You will need to monitor the action of the game carefully, pointing out potential difficulties if players are not sensitive to them and offering suggestions and feedback where needed.

Organize an Intramural, Field-Day Experience, or Olympic Extravaganza

When selected student-generated novel games become the basis of a special event, the efforts of those who engaged in the creative process are acknowledged in a more public venue. This not only brings notoriety to the creators but can be used to enhance public relations, especially if the local media show an interest. Newspapers and television are a natural vehicle for letting others get a glimpse of some of the noteworthy things that are being done in the schools and in community-based recreational settings. If collaborating with a high school or junior high school proves too tedious because of scheduling considerations, one option is to have the creators of the activities introduce their innovative games to younger students in earlier grades, either by having a play day for a given grade, or perhaps by hosting a parent-student night at one of the local elementary schools.

We often are reluctant to try things that are different from the ordinary. We accept the "if it's not broken, don't fix it" attitude. Unfortunately, the price for our reluctance is often an outbreak of the "oh, that again," syndrome. By keeping the tried and true stock but adding variety on occasion, we can keep our physical education and recreation classes vibrant and fresh. Let the games begin!

Evolution of an Innovative Game: A Student's Work in Progress

When an individual or small group is first given an assignment to create an innovative game, reactions are frequently mixed in nature. These range from those who immediately, totally, and happily immerse themselves in the project to those who are bewildered and initially overwhelmed by the challenge, regardless of the extent to which you have prepared them as suggested in chapter 1. Yet, if the instructor is to provide the broadest range of experiences for participants, creation using one or more of the eight principles is required in order to allow the process to come full circle. In doing so, students are not merely passive learners but have a unique opportunity to develop something novel that they can call their own and are, by the very nature of the tasks required, more fully involved in the entire procedure.

Many professionals are at a loss when it comes to assisting others with the development and refinement of their ideas, probably because most have received no formal training in the required steps. The concepts presented in this chapter should assist leaders in understanding their role and in turn help them to realize how to nurture a game from its initial stage to the final product. Additionally, it will provide instructors with the most commonly asked questions and prototypes of responses. The most important factor to keep in mind is that you will serve as facilitator, sounding board, and provider of feedback rather than problem solver. The creation must be the student's not yours, regardless of how obvious the solution might be. Past experiences from attempting to fulfill this role have led me to realize that students often ask similar questions when seeking guidance. I have selected a few of the questions most often asked and provided a prototype response to assist you in working with others to fully develop their creations.

The Most Often Asked Questions

1. *"All of the games have already been invented, so how can you ask us to devise something novel?"*

Have you ever walked down the toy aisles at a store and seen something that was new and different? Of course you have. Well, where do you think the inventor came up with that idea? I suspect that a lot of thought went into the process. Think of all the sports that have been created and later added to the Olympics or the X Games—ice dancing, rhythmic gymnastics, freestyle skiing, skateboarding, and so on. Certainly what you will be creating will probably not be as elaborate and detailed, but who knows what might happen a few decades from now.

2. *"Is it all right if the activity seems very similar to one that already exists?"*

That's perfectly acceptable, but what you really must ask is whether others would see this activity as different enough to be judged a fresh and novel game. For example, ice hockey and roller hockey seem almost identical when you analyze them at their most obvious level, but the distinct locomotor patterns would be interpreted by most to provide enough difference that the two games are seen as separate entities. However, if a volleyball were substituted for a basketball but all rules and actions from basketball were retained, I think most would simply see this as the traditional game. There is no absolute rule I can provide, but if you ask a group of your peers and at least half do not perceive the game as being different from the activity from which it was conceived, then you'll need to go back to the drawing board.

3. *"When I shared with you the idea of moving a Frisbee down the field by throwing and catching to eventually score a goal (or another idea that already existed as a game of which the creator was unaware), I really thought that I had devised an absolutely novel game. Now it's back to square one, right?"*

First, the idea you came up with was innovative within your realm of experience, and you should be proud of yourself. We will play that game at some point, but let's not throw the baby out with the bath water. Let's see if we can use the basic idea of moving an object down the field to score a goal. If you could substitute a different object or use a different method or methods to propel the object, it could result in an innovative activity.

4. *"I've been racking my brain trying to create something, but all I am ever left with is a game that I already know exists. Can you give me a hint?"*

OK, let's start with a game you know, and preferably one that you enjoy. Now consider how the activity (volleyball) would be altered if one of the following occurred. There are normally two teams; what would happen if more were added? Could you substitute equipment that is not traditionally associated with physical education classes? In volleyball, the ball must be sent over the net and all the players from one team are located on that side of the net. What other option might exist for playing the ball? Could you find other ways in which players could score? What would happen if you had players from both teams on each side? Or how might the mobility patterns or use of limbs be modified? What about their effect on the action? Obviously I have given you many ideas to consider. Certainly incorporating one or two concepts and modifying the rules where needed should result in something that will be recognized as different enough from traditional volleyball to be considered novel. Remember, those are merely suggestions, and not all may work. Once you begin to analyze those ideas, I bet you'll realize many other possibilities exist.

Don't feel as if you have to use one of my general ideas; I assure you my feelings won't be hurt in the least.

5. *"I saw this great new toy in a local department store. If we were to buy multiple sets, I could use it as the foundation upon which to base an innovative game. May I do that?"*

Tell me about this equipment and approximately how much it costs. (The student explained that there was a pair of Velcro paddles and Velcro balls that cost approximately $10 per set, with a minimum of 22 people to be outfitted.) Remember one of the requirements that I place on any activity is that the equipment is typically available in most school settings, or can be secured, made or purchased for less than $50. While what you describe seems as if it could work well within the game idea that you shared, it doesn't meet the expense criterion. But let's take a closer look at the equipment you wanted to purchase. Does it really represent a unique way to catch a ball? I bet if you looked in our equipment room, explored the housewares aisles of that department store, or asked 10 people to name different items that you could use to propel and/or catch a ball, you could find one that would make the game novel and still meet our budgetary limits. Why don't you try one of those approaches and share your results with me?

6. *"Why won't you accept a relay or obstacle course as representing an innovative activity?"*

I will accept a game that uses either of those elements as long as it is put into a broader context so that the ultimate goal goes beyond which individual or group is able to complete a task or set of movements before others do so. When this is done, the element of novelty is reintroduced. If not, then I believe most participants will see the activity as a slightly different version of something they probably have done far too often in physical education classes. I will accept a relay or obstacle course if it involves some special or unique feature that distinguishes it from the standard fare. I know that will require some additional analysis on your part, but I'm sure you'll agree that the outcome will be more exciting and will set it apart from all the other relays or obstacle courses you have completed.

7. *"When I was in fourth grade, we played this great game that I had never played before and have never played since. Can I use it?"*

Did you invent this activity? If the response is "yes," and I am not familiar with the game and know of no resource that describes it, I will allow the student to use the game. However, in most circumstances, certain shortcomings or weaknesses are uncovered that require further refinement. If the response is "no," then I share the following: If you didn't formulate the game, then is it really innovative? When you think about it, even though you might not like to admit it, I believe you'll conclude that it isn't really novel. Yet, couldn't the skeleton of the idea and action be preserved, while altering something about the setting, equipment, and/or player configuration to make the game different from its original version? Other possibilities to consider are adding elements or patterns from one of the many standard sports units that most programs offer or adopting aspects from games that receive less exposure such as horseshoes, table tennis, board or lawn darts, shuffleboard, bowling, and the like.

8. *"I thought of this game called "Volley-Baseball." Has anyone ever created an activity like that?"*

It sounds as if it might have possibilities, but often names can be deceiving. There are a number of instances in the past where two or more students have labeled their activities with similar or even identical names, suggesting that they are really clones of one another. However, after they described their creations, I realized that each represented unique contributions. I guess the rule here should be that you can't judge novelty by simply evaluating the name of the game.

No doubt, you have begun to notice some underlying trends or themes. First, be encouraging and positive. Nothing is more devastating to novice game inventors than a curt, patented answer, "It already exists, so go back and try again." Second, try to salvage some elements of the students' original idea. This gives them a foundation from which they can build.

Third, always try to present more than one concept that could be used to modify the initial suggestion. If only one way is offered, then that often narrows thinking by individuals feeling that they must incorporate that particular suggestion. By providing various options for consideration, greater latitude is permitted and individuals realize that there is more than one way to approach the problem. More analysis is required as the multitude of alternatives is weighed and reweighed after the elimination of selected elements.

Fourth, try to avoid providing a specific solution, such as, "If you used a football, you would have a unique creation." Yes, it is often very difficult not to share the obvious, but ask yourself who is supposed to be devising this activity. While not explicit in the answers listed, one excellent technique for those having difficulty with the assigned task is to take an innovative game they have played that parallels a well-known activity and have them tell you specifically how the innovative version differs from its more traditional counterpart. For example, soccer versus Soft Goalball (Lichtman, 1993, pp. 13-15). In Soft Goalball, players use different equipment (gloves and a mushball) and actions (throwing and catching) to move a ball down the field to score a goal. One might suspect that the younger the age group, the more specific the suggestions should be; however, it has been my experience that such generalization does not hold true. I believe the trend is very much individualized and is based upon the extent to which people have been encouraged and rewarded for efforts to think beyond the proverbial box. However, I have found that most younger participants respond well to general suggestions, at times more readily than college-aged students tend to.

Finally, set your parameters ahead of time and be sure that participants understand them. If you do accept a game idea that is borderline relative to the requirements you have imposed, explain to the larger group why you are giving your approval. This will help each to establish a better definition of what is considered novel and innovative.

The Nurturing Process From Inception to the Final Product

The following pages provide the reader with insight into an actual "case history" depicting exactly how the facilitating procedure was applied for a junior Kinesiology major, Terry Wright, who was enrolled in a required innovative games class which met for seven and a half weeks at Sam Houston State University, where I teach. As part of the course's requirements, students must devise an innovative game. The restrictions include the expense and relay/obstacle course parameters alluded to earlier. The activity can be geared for any grade or range of grade levels. As I typically point out, basketball is played by children as young as age seven or eight up through professional players in the NBA and WNBA. The only real differences are in the scale of equipment and generally some modifications in rules, or the strictness with which they are applied. When students are ready, they verbally share their ideas with me.

The Initial Meeting

At our first meeting, Terry asked me if anyone had ever created a game based on horse racing around a track. I responded that I did not recall anyone doing that. Terry was pleased, for this meant there was an excellent chance her idea would be novel. The concept evolved after attending a Renaissance Festival where she'd seen jousting duels on horseback as well as horse-driven cart relay races. She wanted the game to be able to be played by a wide range of ages, but when she thought of a horse and rider, the only thing she could visualize was a preschooler with a wooden horse galloping around. Obviously, that would not work for those above the early elementary grades. Nor did she want participants to be merely running around an oval. After encouraging her to think of alternative means of locomotion she asked if I thought scooters might work, a suggestion with which I concurred.

The next problem to overcome was the jousting, which could be dangerous. After a short discussion we agreed that the specific purpose of jousting was to knock a rider off his horse or, in the broader (and figurative) context, to score points for one's team by temporarily eliminating a participant from continuing play. I asked Terry to think about how other games accomplished this same objective. Her responses included tagging, pulling of flags, and tackling. With prompting from me and by my naming some other sports and activities, she added fouling and being hit with an object, as in bombardment or dodgeball. Tagging and tackling were immediately eliminated because of the potential for rough play and injury. She did not like the notion of fouling, as that occurred as a byproduct of the action and was not the intent of the game. The use of flagbelts was carefully considered but dropped as the ends might get entangled in the wheels, and even worse, someone's fingers might be run over if that person reached for the end of a flag that was touching the floor. The only option left was to be hit by a ball. Terry liked that element, as dodging activities have universal appeal and pose almost no threat of injury when foam-type balls like those we play with during class are used. Such foam balls appear as standard issue throughout the activities in *Innovative Games* and *More Innovative Games*. Thus at the conclusion of our initial meeting, which lasted no more than four or five minutes, it was decided that the game would involve students on scooters circling an oval track, while members from other teams attempted to hit them with foam-type balls. That provided the framework of the activity, leaving Terry to work out the rest of the details. I encourage thinking about safety issues and always stress that a reasonable number of students should be active simultaneously in a typically-sized space. This is critical, as physical educators often are expected to keep large classes fully engaged in facilities of limited size.

The Second Meeting

In keeping with the horse-and-rider theme, Terry decided that a jump rope or piece of rope should be tied around the waists of the individual on the scooter, who would serve as the rider, and another person who would be upright and pulling, simulating a horse. I liked the concept but asked if she had tested this means of locomotion. She had not but promised she would do so before our next meeting and let me know the result.

I realized that such a configuration would not work but felt it best to let her discover this for herself since this was her creation, not mine. It was Terry who would have to come up with a possible solution.

She realized that a true oval was just too hard to simulate, so a basketball court seemed like the closest natural area, as the horses and riders could travel in the space outside of the side- and endlines. That left the court itself to position the opposing team, from which they would throw balls.

I asked if there were any restrictions put on those who were throwing. She indicated that they had to hit the riders below head level for a point to be scored. My intent was really to probe whether the throwers could roam over the entire court, which would be no contest, or whether a throwing zone had been defined. I would return to that aspect after I first inquired whether the horses could be hit also. Terry hadn't considered that but believed it would add to the game and decided to include them as targets. When I asked her to clarify the awarding of points, she first said that one point would be earned if either a rider or horse were hit, but when hits had been scored on both the rider and the horse from a specific pair, they had to leave the game. Innocently, I asked what would be accomplished by having pairs of people sitting on the sidelines. Without ever really responding to my question, she realized that would defeat the purpose of keeping participants active and retracted that rule, opting to merely keep track of points. "Is it equally as difficult to hit a horse as a rider?" I inquired. Her response was, "No, the horses have more ability to dodge, but I guess a rider could purposefully fall off her horse to avoid being hit." When I wondered aloud whether that should make a difference in the number of points awarded, Terry settled on two points for hitting a horse, one point for hitting a rider while on the scooter, and one point each time the rider fell off the scooter.

Again I asked about a thrower's ability to move about the court. After some thought, Terry decided to set up a 45-foot (13.7-meter) throwing line that was centered within the court, with the endpoints marked by cones, leaving approximately 22 feet (6.7 meters) from either end to an endline. Thus, throwers were required to project the balls about 25 to 27 feet (7.6 to 8.2 meters) to hit one of the moving targets.

This give-and-take process continued with the following things decided at this 10-minute session: the size and number of balls (six softball-sized balls); how to keep the horses and riders from cutting the corners of the "track" (place a cone at each corner); how many pairs of horses and riders would be active at once (six; action starts with two equally spread out on each sideline, and one in the middle of each endline), and how the game would flow and end. (Throwers can retrieve balls but must return to the throwing line before aiming at the participants, who continue to circle the track counterclockwise for three minutes until the inning is over. A game consists of six or nine innings in which each team faces every other team two or three times, respectively.)

The Third Meeting

Terry admitted her idea about tying the rope around the waist was a disaster but solved the problem by having the rider hold the ends of a seven- to eight-foot (2.1- to 2.4-meter) jump rope while the horse grips the rope in the middle using one hand as depicted in figure 2.1.

She also realized that if the playing area could not be enlarged for grades five and above, she would have to make it harder to hit the targets by requiring throwers to use their non-preferred hand, or self-drop the ball striking it with a palm or fist. The dilemma of how to keep track of the scoring was solved through the use of a third team serving as referees, which she had seen employed within a number of innovative games where the action is continuous and spread over the entire facility.

Terry's final product, which she called Bombardment Derby, did not address the exact positioning of the 12 referees, nor did it provide an adequate description of how the score for a particular inning was to be determined. Yet, within three meetings that lasted a total of 19 to 20 minutes, the makings of a game were solidified, with the majority of the weaknesses addressed. Subsequent feedback that I provided on her assignment suggested that the officials might be handled as follows: each

Figure 2.1 Simulated horse and rider with the horse attempting to dodge a ball.

seated referee records points for hits and for riders who fall off their scooters at the specific end of the track or on a given half of the sideline toward which that official is facing. To avoid interference in play, these six individuals should sit on the court about 12 feet (3.7 meters) inside the side- or endline. The other six judges stand and face the throwers, ready to record points for any hits on which a violation occurred. Two of these standing officials are spread out over each side of the court, one is positioned at each end of the track, and all are at least nine feet (2.7 meters) beyond the nearest line. An illustration of Terry's original sketch, along with the suggested positioning of the referees, can be seen in figure 2.2.

After each inning, the seated and standing judges meet independently to total the points that were earned in their specific section of the court. The inning's score for the teams of horses and riders is determined by subtracting the standing judges' total from that of the seated referees. The winning team is determined by the fewest number of points scored.

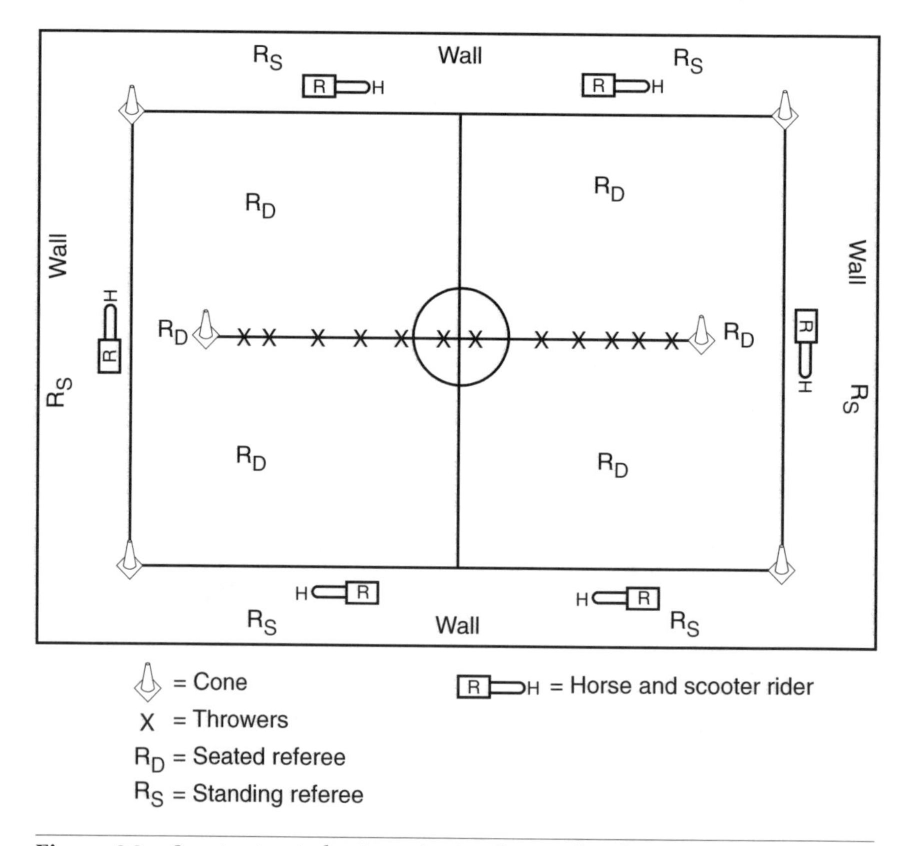

Figure 2.2 Court setup to begin an inning for Bombardment Derby.

Subsequent Changes

Other classes have since incorporated additional modifications to Bombardment Derby. Among the most noteworthy changes are the following:

- If any horse and her rider can avoid being hit during an entire inning, five points is added to the standing officials' total.
- Riders are provided with a badminton racket, which can be used to redirect a ball's path.
- Throwers may not step over the end- or sidelines to retrieve a ball that is located between those lines and the walls. The closest standing referee will return the ball to the playing surface of the court.
- To discourage cheating, the standing judges' point total is doubled.
- The appropriate sitting judge records two points if a horse purposely drops his end of the rope to avoid being hit.

It seems that each time this game is played, additional ideas for changes are forthcoming and encouraged. This helps students understand that just as "Rome wasn't built in a day," the best creations are ones that evolve over time. All the readers who are wondering how young adults can enjoy Bombardment Derby have a standing invitation to attend my innovative games classes. The true test comes from students who complain if I fail to offer them the opportunity to play Bombardment Derby, or any number of other novel creations.

Developing Hybrid Activities

When you merge elements from two or more standard activities, the resulting product is a different game than those from which you borrowed. This approach for devising innovative curricular offerings is not only easy to understand, but the possibilities are almost limitless.

The simplest way to visualize potential pairings is to draw a matrix similar to the one in table 3.1. The horizontal and vertical axes represent well-known sports.

Although the combinations identified in table 3.1 either have been developed or appear to be promising, obviously not all combinations are feasible. For example, if you merged volleyball and field hockey and required players to use a field hockey stick to propel a volleyball over a net, the game might not be successful. If chapter 7, which discusses modified uses of standard equipment, suggested playing field hockey with a

Table 3.1

Schema for Developing Hybrid Activities

Well-known sport	Softball	Basketball	Volleyball	Soccer
Softball	—	Soft-basket	Soft-volley	Soft-goalball*
Basketball	—	—	Basket-volley	Spasketball*
Volleyball	—	—	—	Volley-soccer*
Soccer	—	—	—	—

*Based on data from *Innovative Games* (Lichtman, 1993, pp. 13-15, 17-22).

volleyball, the result would not be considered a hybrid activity because major elements from volleyball haven't been infused into the game.

Table 3.1 is not meant to be exhaustive; rather, it is intended to provide a conceptual method for creating hybrid activities. Furthermore, table 3.1 only includes pairs of sports. Very often, elements from a third activity can, or in some cases must, be integrated in order to refine the new creation.

The Games

The activities in this chapter are arranged in a degree-of-difficulty continuum, from simple to complex. A number of skills incorporated within the last three games, Flag Basketball, Soccer Flag Football, and Multi-Option Ball tend to reinforce each other, but subtle rule changes might result in inappropriate transfer from game to game. To reduce this possibility, instructors should not introduce these consecutively.

SOCCER CROQUET—FOUR WAYS

Using soccer actions to send a ball through a series of consecutively numbered wickets, four different activities emerge. One is evaluated by number of kicks (for a slower-paced activity). A second variation is judged by the amount of time elapsed, and a third is assessed by a combination of the number of kicks and the elapsed time required to complete the course (each results in a faster version). A fourth variation involves a team's attempts to kick a soccer ball through its preset sequence of wickets while preventing an opposing team from being the first to successfully complete its designated wicket course.

Objectives

Reinforce soccer skills; in the faster paced and the team versions, improve agility, speed, and cardiorespiratory endurance.

Equipment

In versions one, two, and three, when individualized competition is taking place, for one-quarter to one-half of a class of 30 to 40 to be active at the same time, 10 soccer balls, volleyballs, or utility balls plus 25 wickets and five cones are recommended so five identical stations can be set up. In paired competition, only five balls are required.

Wickets can be created by unbending two wire hangers, twisting together an end of each hanger, forming a half circle, and then inserting the ends into the dirt. Another option is to cut a hula hoop in half and insert the ends into the holes of a brick. Each wicket is numbered by folding a sheet of paper in half, stapling the free sides, printing a number with a magic marker, and sliding the paper over one end of the wicket.

Versions two and three also require at least one watch with a stopwatch function per station (preferably two watches would be used). Version four requires 20 wickets, with five sets numbered one through four; 20 cones; pinnies for two-thirds of the participants, with equal numbers of three different colors; strips of white cloth, each approximately 5 by 48 inches (0.13 by 1.2 meters) for one-third of the players; a pair of index cards per station, each with one of two different orders of wicket completion listed; and two soccer balls per station, preferably each with different colored panels.

Playing Area

A large grassy field measuring at least 60 by 100 yards (54.9 by 91.4 meters).

Participants

For each station, six or eight participants for versions one through three. For version four, assign either six or nine per station. Participants serve as referees.

Game

Variations one through three possess a number of common features, including a five wicket layout per station as seen in figure 3.1. Separate consecutive wickets by at least 50 yards (45.7 meters). Players waiting their turn line up behind the cone on the side away from the action. When a player or a partner puts the ball through wicket #3, the next person(s) should begin the course. After successfully negotiating the

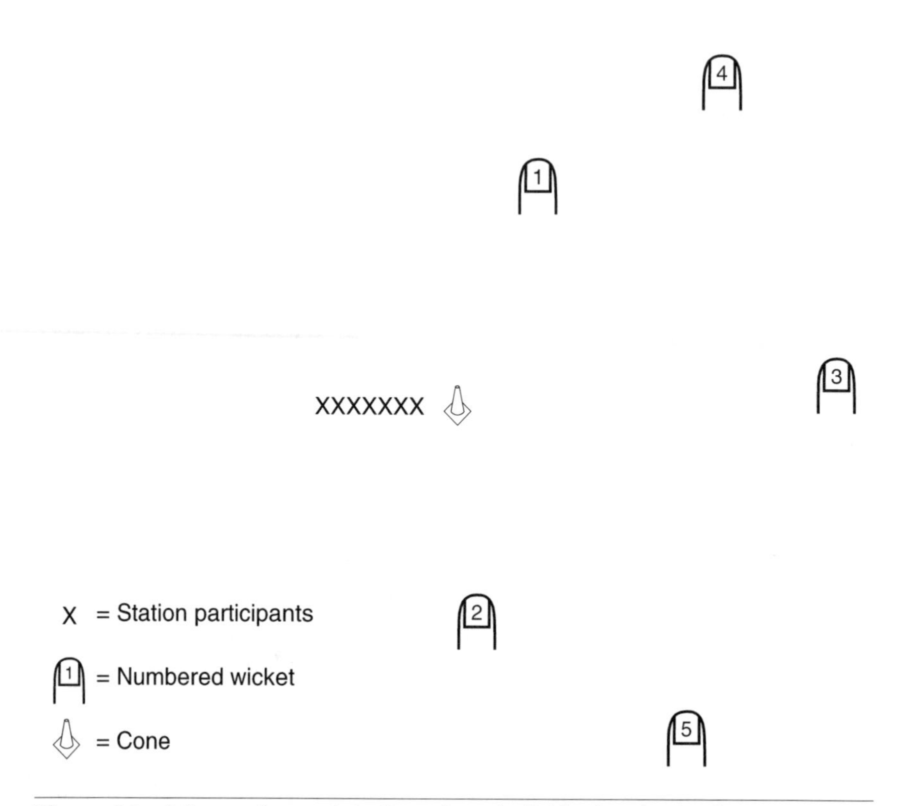

Figure 3.1 A Soccer Croquet station where individual and paired competition occurs based upon the number of kicks, time, or a combination of both contacts and time.

fifth wicket, the ball must strike the cone for the action to be complete. Should the ball be kicked through a wicket that is out of sequence, the player(s) must go back and complete the missed wicket, and then each of the following wickets in proper order. It is immaterial in which direction the ball is sent through the wicket. Upon finishing the course, the player(s) should join at the end of their station's line. When partners work together they must alternate kicking the ball. Each time a player contacts the ball twice in succession, a two-kick or 10-second penalty is applied to the pair's score.

Version One

Number of Kicks. With single-person competition, have another student run along and count the number of contacts. Switch tasks when these players are again at the front of the line at their station. With pairs who are each kicking, assign another pair to run the course, with one counting the number of kicks and the other watching for violations.

Version Two

Time. Follow a procedure similar to that outlined in version one except that the individual who was tallying the number of kicks now will be giving feedback on the amount of time elapsed.

Version Three

Time and Number of Kicks. The flow is the same as version two; however, the number of kicks is multiplied by five and added to the number of seconds it took to complete the course. Remember to convert properly to minutes and seconds; e.g., for 20 kicks, with a running time of 3:04, the recorded score after conversion would be 4:44.

Version Four

Simultaneous Offensive and Defensive Play. Divide the class into teams of two or three players with three teams assigned to a station. At each station, four wickets are positioned in a square with 20 to 30 yards (18.3 to 27.4 meters) between them, depending upon the participants' skills, and a cone is located five yards (4.6 meters) in back of each wicket, as shown in figure 3.2.

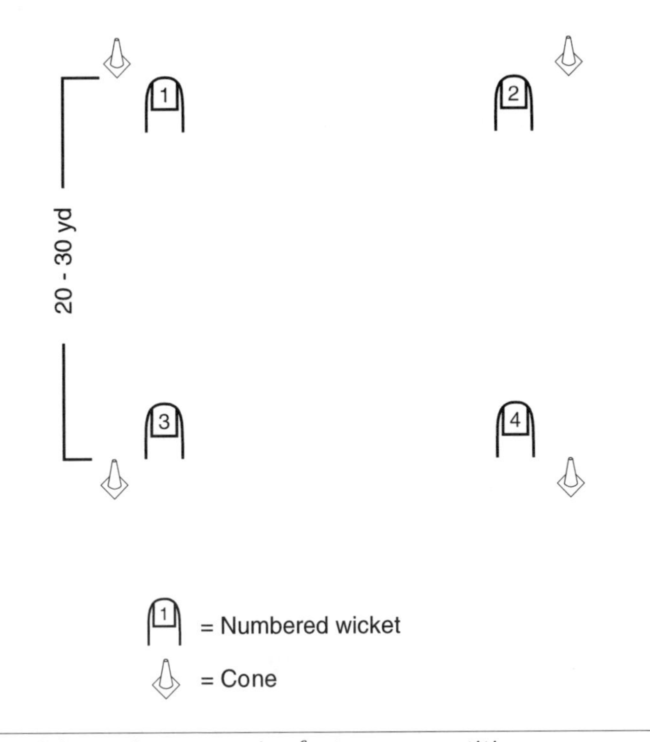

Figure 3.2 A Soccer Croquet station for team competition.

Each team must identify the order in which its players will contact the ball. A pinnie of a given color is worn by the first player to contact the ball, the second wears a different color, and if a team includes a third player, that person wears the remaining color. To assist the referees, base the pinnie color assignment on some logical order such as the colors of the rainbow, with red going to person one, blue to the second individual, and so on, or in alphabetical order with say, blue given to the first person to contact the ball, green to the second, and so on. Since competing teams will be wearing the identical pinnie colors, one group of three should tie a white cloth strip around each of their waists.

One team and its referee is given a wicket sequence of 4-2-3-1, while the other team and referee receive 1-3-2-4, or similar configuration where the wickets on opposite sides of the square are completed by each team before the team traverses to the next cone diagonally across the square. Sequences are written on an index card and kept by the referee. When nine players are assigned to a station, the ninth individual can assist the other referees in calling violations. Each team attempts to be the first to complete its wicket sequence correctly while preventing the other team from doing so; however, the players from each team must alternate who plays the ball according to the predetermined order, and all individuals on both teams may play the ball for no more than five seconds consecutively.

Violations

The next wicket in sequence is awarded to the opposing team when a player

a. kicks the team's ball out of proper sequence,
b. kicks the opponent's ball while standing outside of the coned square,
c. plays a ball for more than five seconds consecutively, or
d. commits a standard soccer infraction.

If a player contacts the ball so that it inadvertently hits a member out of sequence from either his team or the opposing team, no violation results so long as that player did not and does not attempt to play the ball. The contact sequence for a team does not begin with the player who was inadvertently contacted; instead, the original order resumes.

Additional Rules

The game begins with each team positioned at the cone that is diagonally opposite the first wicket they must complete. Players who are waiting their turn to compete serve as referees. A referee focuses on her assigned team's ball, recording violations made when the ball is in play. Additionally, the official tracks the number of consecutive seconds a player has been playing the ball, beginning the count aloud at the three-second mark. Every time a team successfully puts the ball through the appropriate wicket, or a wicket has been awarded because of a violation, the referee of that team must announce aloud the wicket number that has been awarded/completed and the next wicket to which the team should be headed.

Helpful Hints

Remind players that the awarding of a wicket is a costly penalty. A referee can assist the team he is watching by calling the pinnie color of the player who should contact the team's ball next. Strategy dictates that the player who last played her team's ball will attempt, whenever possible, to secure the opposing team's ball and kick it as far as possible away from the next wicket to which her team will be headed. If successful, this will force the player from the opposing team who must next contact the ball to run a long distance. The first time this game is attempted, players tend to be more concerned with making progress with their own team's wickets than trying to knock the other team's ball away. While this reduces the strategic nature of this activity, players will still view this as innovative. However, once participants are comfortable with the alternating order of play, they will apply defensive tactics when crossing paths in the middle of the wicket square.

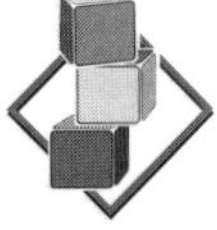

Adaptations for Younger Participants

Prohibit opposing players from kicking the ball away. Add a stipulation that should the order of play rule, the five-second consecutive play rule, or the hand ball rule be violated, the person committing the transgression must complete a lap, outside of the cones, before that individual may play the ball again.

DODGE BASKETBALL

Incorporate elements of dodgeball while playing basketball and an exciting game is created. The resulting activity requires participants to use shielding strategies to protect the member of their team who has control of the ball.

Objectives

Reinforces basketball and throwing skills; enhances agility, speed, and cardiorespiratory endurance.

Equipment

One basketball, four to eight soccer-size foam balls, and seven to nine pinnies per court.

Playing Area

A basketball court with an area of at least five feet (1.5 meters) beyond each sideline and endline.

Participants

Seven to nine players per team with five courts and two to four sideline players per team, plus two referees per court.

Game

As seen in figure 3.3, one or two sideline players from a given team are positioned on the half of the court nearest their team's basket, while a like number from the same team are on the other sideline diagonally across on the half of the court closest to where their team defends the basket. Sideline players are permitted to move along their entire half of the sideline, but may not go behind either endline or cross to their opponents' portions of the sidelines unless they commit a violation and must run around the outside of the basketball court.

Each sideline player begins the game with one foam ball. Typical basketball action occurs except as noted below. Sideline players attempt to hit the member of the opposing team who has control of the basketball (fig-

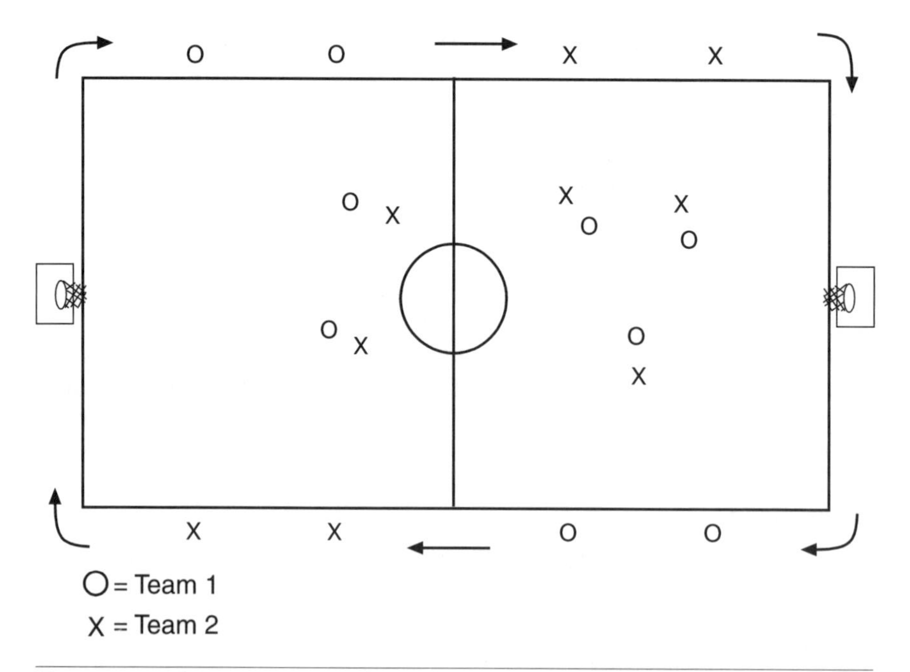

Figure 3.3 Player positioning for Dodge Basketball and the route court players must take when circling the court after being hit at waist level or below.

ure 3.4). If that player is hit at the waist or below while he has control of the ball, a member of the other team puts the ball into play at the spot on the court where the opponent was hit. The court player who was hit must exit by the nearest endline and run clockwise around the outside of the court, without interfering with sideline players or again getting hit at the waist or below, before re-entering the court at the spot where he originally left. Should the runner be hit while in the area behind one of the endlines or while traversing the territories where sideline players from his team are positioned, no consequences occur. However, if the runner gets hit by an opposing team's sideline player while traversing an opposing sideline area, the player continues to run until successfully negotiating a complete lap without being hit. Note, a lap always begins and ends at the endline location where the player initially left the court. Should a foam ball contact a court player who does not have control of the ball, play continues.

Figure 3.4 Action in Dodge Basketball where a sideline player is trying to hit a shooter from the opposing team with a foam ball before the shot is released. If successful, the shooter must complete one lap clockwise around the outside of the court without getting hit while traversing the sideline areas defended by the opposing team.

Foam balls that remain on the court may only be retrieved by court players, who must use their feet to propel the balls to the sideline players. A runner may kick a foam ball that is located beyond the endline or their team's sideline areas without penalty. However, if either a court player or a runner uses his hands to secure or touch a foam ball, he must complete a lap, or an extra lap in the case of a runner, without being hit by the opposing team's sideline players in the sideline areas in which those individuals are defending.

If a player is hit at the waist or below while shooting but before the ball has left the shooter's hand, any basket made doesn't count and the opposing team takes over at the spot where the shot was taken. If a player shooting a free throw is hit at the waist or below, a point is awarded to the shooting team regardless of whether the shot was successful. Sideline players are permitted to throw the foam balls to each other, but since there is no penalty if a foam ball hits a sideline player, it is illogical for opposing teams' sideline players to aim at each other or at runners from the other team that are located on their team's sideline areas. Should a sideline player step onto the court, go into either endline area or the opposing team's sideline area, or throw a ball while a free throw is being taken, she must drop any foam balls and become a runner who must successfully complete a trip around the court without being hit as described previously. After four to five minutes of play, two court players switch with the sideline players.

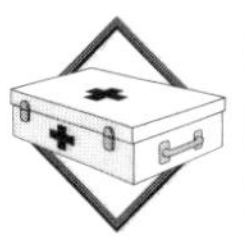

Safety Considerations

Remind sideline players that balls must hit at the waist or below to be considered good. While there is a possibility for a court player to step on a foam ball, the probability of an injury is remote.

Helpful Hints

Discuss the strategy of using offensive team players who don't have control of the ball as shields when shots are taken on the side of the court where the opposing team's sideline players are located. Additionally, sideline players should alert court players so that loose foam balls can be kicked to them. When a player has been hit, the opposing team is at a tremendous advantage playing five on four, and the longer a team can delay the runner's return as a court player, the better.

Both referees observe the actions that take place on the court, including contacts by foam balls, until there is at least one runner. As determined in advance, one of the referees will concentrate on the actions directed at the runner(s) by the opposing sideline players. After a violation, one of these officials should blow a whistle to signal when the ball is put in play, alerting participants to the fact that hits by foam balls will be counted. The other referee continues to observe the action on the court.

FLAG BASKETBALL

Executing basketball skills within the context of a flag football setting while providing different options for scoring results in a fast-paced strategic game.

Objectives

Develops basketball dribbling and passing skills, enhances agility and speed, reinforces many rules of flag football.

Equipment

For each game, one soccer ball, 14 to 16 flag belts, seven to eight pinnies, two pieces of rope, each three feet (0.9 meter) in length, and two hula hoops suspended from the cross bar of one goal post.

Playing Area

From the 40-yard (36.6-meter) line of a football field to the back of the end zone on the same side of the field. Two games may occur simultaneously on one football field.

Participants

Fourteen to 16 players and two referees per game.

Game

Divide the players into two different teams. Play begins in the traditional fashion of flag football, but the offense starts from the 40-yard (36.6-meter) line. The flow of the game is similar to flag football; however, participants are not allowed to run with the ball, but must dribble basketball-style to make forward progress. The only exception to this rule is for the quarterback, who may run with the ball as long as he is behind the line of scrimmage; however, he must dribble once that line is crossed. Play is stopped when the player who has control of the ball has her flag stolen; the ball is kicked, with the exception of a field goal or point after; a forward pass is dropped; the defense secures the ball after a fumble; or the ball is sent out-of-bounds. A team is permitted to complete one forward pass per play from a player who is in front of the line of scrimmage, unless the team is attempting a two-point conversion after a touchdown has been scored. In such a case, there is no limit to the number of forward passes that may be completed. The offensive team is allowed four plays to advance at least 20 yards (18.3 meters) beyond the line of scrimmage or score, whichever comes first (figure 3.5).

Figure 3.5 Start of a play in Flag Basketball. The quarterback is lateraling to a teammate while an opponent is trying to stop the play by pulling the quarterback's flag before the ball is pitched. Upon receiving the ball, the player will need to pass the ball either forward or backward or use a basketball dribble to bring the ball down the field.

A touchdown and a field goal are worth six and three points, respectively. After a touchdown, the point after may be scored by a player standing in the field of play and throwing the ball through one of the hoops or kicking the ball through the uprights. A two-point conversion requires the offense to run a play and throw the ball through one of the hoops while the shooter is standing within the end zone. Note, this shot may be taken while the person is located in back of the hoops, and there is no limit to the number of forward passes that may be completed on this given play.

Play begins at the 40-yard (36.6-meter) line if the defense successfully recovers a fumble, a fumbled ball goes out-of-bounds off a defender, or a field goal or point after is awarded. If two games are taking place on the same field, the farthest back any team should be penalized for infractions is to the 50-yard (45.7-meter) line.

Violations

If a second forward pass beyond the line of scrimmage occurs on a given play, other than on a two-point conversion, the team is penalized five yards (4.6 meters) or half of the distance to the goal from the point where the second pass was thrown.

Traveling and double dribbling, as defined in basketball, result in a five-yard (4.6-meter) penalty or half of the distance to the goal from the spot of the violation.

On a non-passing play or after an offensive player has gained control of the ball from a pass, if the ball goes out-of-bounds, the team that last touched it retains possession.

Kicking the ball is only permitted on a field goal or point after. Soccer-style dribbling or passing (with the feet) to move the ball down the field is not permitted. A five-yard (4.6-meter) penalty or half of the distance to the goal is assessed from the spot of the violation.

A player is not allowed to purposely throw the ball at a player's legs, causing that individual to inadvertently kick the ball. A five-yard (4.6-meter) penalty or half of the distance to the goal occurs from the spot of the foul.

Interference on a passing play results in a five-yard (4.6-meter) penalty or half of the distance to the goal from where the transgression occurred.

Excessively rough or dangerous play should be penalized by 10 yards (9.1 meters) or half of the distance to the goal with the offensive team beginning a new set of downs.

Safety Considerations

Since basketball shots may be taken from the back of the end zone, extra care should be used around that location by placing padding around the portion of the goal post that is anchored into the ground.

Players have a tendency to kick the ball after a fumble. To prevent this, remind participants that the only time the ball may be kicked is for a field goal or point after.

Helpful Hints

The one forward pass beyond the line of scrimmage is especially useful when a person is in danger of having his flag taken. To avoid a second pass violation, encourage the thrower of the forward pass to yell out "no pass" once the ball is released.

SOCCER FLAG FOOTBALL

By crossing soccer-style play with the general rules of flag football, an exciting and faster-paced version of the gridiron game emerges. In this hybrid game, players have the option of scoring into a net by kicking or throwing a football, or by completing a touchdown when playing with a football.

Objectives

Develops flag football skills, soccer-style dribbling and kicking, speed, agility, and cardiorespiratory endurance.

Equipment

One foam football, 11 pinnies, and 20 flagbelts (none needed for goalies).

Playing Area

A football field.

Participants

Eleven players per team and two referees per field.

Game

Action begins as in soccer, and whenever the ball is on the ground, even after a missed catch, it must be played with the feet, except for the goalie, who may pick up the ball directly from the ground within her end zone. However, should the ball be propelled directly from a body part and be caught in the air, it may be played with the hands, by lateraling, passing, or kicking, or the player may advance the ball by running (figure 3.6). The team without the ball may stop play by pulling the flag of the person who has the ball in her arms or hands. Pulling a flag serves no purpose if the ball is on the ground or in the air. Once play is stopped, the line of scrimmage is established at that point, and teams line up in typical football fashion and run a play after the ball is hiked. Where the ball is located on the field dictates which player positions will be involved in the action, as seen in table 3.2.

On any play, only two people are permitted to stay in and block for the quarterback, and neither these individuals nor the quarterback is eligible to receive or run the ball unless it has been touched by some other player. A team that runs three consecutive plays without the ball hitting the ground must have advanced the ball at least 10 yards (9.1 meters) beyond the line of scrimmage or else the opposing team

Figure 3.6 Trying to loft the ball to a teammate in Soccer Flag Football so play can continue using the hands rather than the feet.

Table 3.2

Player Position Involvement at Specific Field Locations

Location	Player positions involved
Between the 20-yard lines	Forward and halfbacks from both teams
Inside the opposing team's 20-yard line	Offensive team's forward line and the defensive team's halfbacks, fullbacks, and goalie (who must play in his/her own end zone)

takes over. However, once the ball hits the playing surface, a new line of scrimmage will be established at the point where the player who gained control of the ball with his hands had his flag stolen.

Scoring occurs when a ball is propelled into the area immediately below the uprights by throwing (one point) or by kicking (two points), provided the ball was released before crossing the goal line. A touchdown and safety, as defined in the traditional game of football, are awarded two points and one point respectively, but safeties can't be called on the goalie.

Violations

If a player is in an area in which she is not permitted, play stops, a 10-yard (9.1-meter) penalty is assessed (or half of the distance to the goal from the spot of the violation), and a first down is awarded.

Pass interference results in a 10-yard (9.1-meter) penalty from the line of scrimmage (or half of the distance to the goal), and a first down is awarded.

Unduly rough play is penalized 15 yards (13.7 meters) from the line of scrimmage (or half of the distance to the goal).

Additional Rules

Once a goalie secures the ball in the end zone, all opposing team players must leave the end zone and return to the field of play. Action resumes when the goalie throws or kicks the ball.

If a ball is kicked out-of-bounds over a sideline, the opposing team gains possession at the yard line where the ball went out, but in the center of the field widthwise. The ball is put back in play football-style.

If a field player picks up the ball directly from the ground, possession of the ball goes to the opposing team, which then puts the ball in play football-style.

Once a ball carrier's flag is pulled, play stops, and the line of scrimmage is established at that point. It is legal for a player whose flag is about to get pulled to kick, dribble, or pass the ball forward or backward, as would be the case in soccer.

Safety Considerations

Initially, upon an incomplete pass, players will have a tendency to think the play is dead, or when the ball is fumbled, they will attempt to pick up the ball and run. In either of these instances, if a referee yells "soccer play," these lapses will be minimized.

Helpful Hints

Participants already should possess some general flag football skills before engaging in Soccer Flag Football. Additionally, separate practice will be needed for self-lofting and for lifting the football from the turf to others using the feet.

MULTI-OPTION BALL

By simultaneously using a football and a soccer ball, expanding the possibilities for scoring, and not permitting a player to directly pick up one of the balls from the ground, a fast-paced game incorporating kicking, passing, and dribbling skills results.

Objectives

Develops selected soccer and football style skills, enhances cardiorespiratory endurance, speed, and agility.

Equipment

One foam football, one foam soccer ball, 14 pinnies, and chalk or polyspots to indicate scoring zones.

Playing Area

A soccer field, with two soccer goals. Figure 3.7 shows the positioning of the scoring zones. Each zone is 12 feet (3.7 meters) in diameter. Each of the four zone ones are 37 feet (11.3 meters) from the endline with the center of the circle located 12 feet (3.7 meters) on a 45 degree diagonal from the corner of the goal area. Each zone two is centered with a net, and the edge closest to the goal is 30 feet (9.1 meters) from the front side of the goal area.

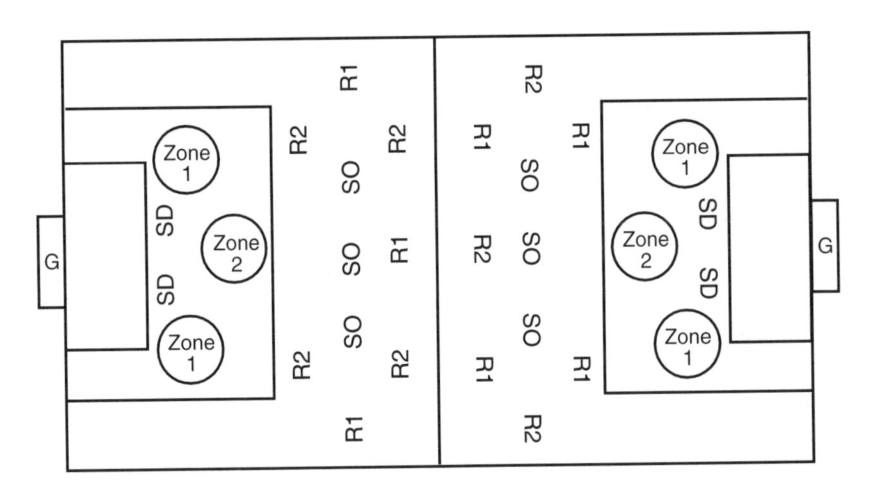

Figure 3.7 Court design for Multi-Option Ball.

Participants

Each team consists of 12 to 14 players: one goalie, two to three defensive players who remain on their team's half of the field, two to three offensive players who stay on the opposing team's half of the field, and six to seven players who run the full length of the field and play both offense and defense. There are two referees. One follows the play of the football, while the other tracks the soccer ball.

Game

The action is much like that of speedaway in that both the football and soccer ball can be played with the feet or with the hands, provided that a participant other than the goalie has not directly picked up or touched the ball as it rebounds directly from the grass. Thus, a basketball-type dribble is eliminated for all players except the goalie. Should either ball fall to the turf, a player would be required to either tip the ball up to himself or to another player who must catch the ball in the air before it can be played with the hands.

Scoring options are outlined in table 3.3.

The game begins with one of the balls in each of the goalies' hands, as decided in an arbitrary fashion. Goalie play is similar to that in soccer as goalies are the only players allowed to pick up a ball directly from the

Table 3.3

Scoring Possibilities in Multi-Option Ball

Ball	Location of shot	Motor pattern	Points
Football	Not in a zone	Kick ball on ground	2
Football	Not in a zone	Throw	1
Soccer ball	Not in a zone	Kick ball on ground	2
Soccer ball	Not in a zone	Throw	1
Football	Zone one	Throw	2
Football	Zone one	Kick any manner	3
Soccer ball	Zone one	Throw	2
Soccer ball	Zone one	Kick any manner	4
Football	Zone two	Throw	3
Football	Zone two	Kick any manner	4
Soccer ball	Zone two	Throw	4
Soccer ball	Zone two	Kick any manner	5

ground. Other players who receive a pass that is caught in the air are allowed up to four steps to come to a stop. Once a player has established a position other than as an offensive player in one of her team's zones, she is permitted the same locomotor action as in basketball.

Only one offensive player is permitted in a zone at a time, and the defense is not permitted to enter into any of the opponent's zones. Incidental transgression by the defense into these zones is not called unless the offense is put at a distinct disadvantage. If a shot on goal is made from an opponent's zone, points will be awarded only if the ball had been passed from another player and caught on the fly by an offensive player who was positioned in that zone immediately prior to the shot being taken. Once the ball is secured by an offensive player in an opponent's zone, he has 10 seconds to get the ball out of the zone but is allowed to move freely within that zone. After a score, or after the ball is returned to a front corner of the goal, the goalie has 30 seconds to put the ball into play. The goalie should do this quickly unless there is danger of a score occurring with the other ball. Should the ball be sent beyond the endline, regardless of which team last touched the ball, a member of the offensive team must retrieve the ball. If the offense had touched it last, the ball is returned to one of the front corners of the goal for the goalie to put the ball into play; if last contacted by the defense, the ball is put into play by the offense at the junction of the nearest endline and sideline as rapidly as possible.

Violations

For any of the following violations, a change of possession occurs at the spot of the infraction, or on the line surrounding that zone should the offensive transgression occur in one of that team's zones:

- Picking up or touching the ball with the hands after it rebounds directly from the playing surface, with the exception of the goalie while he is in his goal box.
- Unduly rough play.
- Traveling with the ball, with the exception of an offensive player in her zone. (Outside of a zone, the same stepping pattern as used in basketball is applied once position is established with the ball held in a player's hands.)
- A ball goes over a sideline.
- Two offensive players are in one zone simultaneously, provided the offense gains the advantage.
- An offensive player runs the ball into a zone.
- An offensive player in a zone lofts or tips the ball to himself.

Additional Rules

A penalty shot is awarded from any zone of the individual's choosing using the same ball that was in play when the violation occurred. Note, when a penalty shot is taken, all play on the field ceases until the goalie puts that ball into play, regardless of the result of the penalty shot. Penalty shots are awarded for each of the following violations:

- A defensive player, other than the goalie, uses her hands to stop a goal shot that is on the ground or has just rebounded from the playing surface.
- Excessively rough play by the defense when either ball is within a goalie's box.
- Failure of a goalie to put the ball into play within 30 seconds after a goal has been scored or after the ball is returned to a front corner of the goal by the offensive player whose team had sent it over the endline.

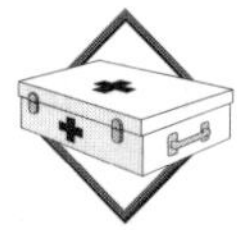

Safety Considerations

The no-pickup rule is important, as injuries can easily occur should a player inappropriately transfer action after a fumble in football to Multi-Option Ball and inadvertently be kicked by another individual who is correctly playing the ball with his feet. If the area in front of the goal becomes very congested, consider limiting kicking into the goal to balls that are on the ground, thus eliminating the drop kick or the kicking of hand-held balls.

Helpful Hints

Person-to-person guarding is required. Similar strategies that are used in football, basketball, and soccer should be applied. Before competition begins, be sure participants practice self-lofts with both balls and lofting the football to another player. The many options for scoring are difficult for players to remember at first. It is easier for players to realize that for any location, throwing is awarded fewer points than kicking, and the further you are away from the goal, the more the score is worth. For less highly skilled players, the zones may be moved closer to the goal, and if a second goalie is needed, use one less defender.

Adaptations for Younger Participants

Add a second goalie and eliminate the zones until participants have had enough experience with the game to be familiar with the general flow of the action. When the zones are included, use only the four zone ones, and position each within about 25 to 30 feet (7.6 to 9.1 meters) from the goal. By omitting zones two, middle-of-the-field crowding will be reduced.

Creating Excitement With Nontraditional Equipment

New activities emerge when equipment or materials not typically associated with sports become the focal point around which a game is developed. The adage "One person's trash is another person's treasure" certainly applies to the activities in this chapter.

Be a collector of odds and ends if your storage facilities allow and even if you don't see an immediate use for the objects. What things should you save? Save:

- plastic and foam cups;
- foam pellets used for packing breakable objects;
- cans, bowls, or containers of varying sizes, all made from unbreakable material;
- bottle caps;
- carpet squares;
- old towels and sheets;
- pieces of excess material;
- balloons;
- broken equipment that can be handled safely;
- tennis ball cans;
- shuttlecock tubes;
- crumpled pieces of paper and aluminum foil;
- spoons;
- spatulas;
- wood;
- rope and string;
- toilet plungers;
- and the like.

The list of nontraditional equipment that could be used in activities is endless. More difficult than finding materials is deciding how to incorporate them into an innovative game. Let your imagination run wild!

Because most games involve projecting an object toward a target and/or catching that object, you should ask how your newly acquired treasure could be used for those purposes. If there is no obvious answer, consider whether the equipment could serve as a boundary marker or the target. In many instances, different action patterns will be needed to execute required movements when using unusual equipment. For example, when a bottomless jug is used to throw a ball, overhand actions require a drastically shortened backswing to prevent the ball from dropping behind the player.

The Games

The activities within this chapter are arranged according to the extent to which they require specialized skills which must be taught and for which students should gain reasonable proficiency before engaging in competition. The first two games, Bottlecap Golf and Volley-Tennis Broom Ball, can be infused immediately. Usually Sheetball Brigade is picked up quite quickly, and the skill acquired in propelling a ball on a sheet should readily carry over to the motions needed to project a ball from a towel, required in Towel Ball Pin Bombardment. Milk Jug Football is the most demanding from a skills perspective, requiring throwing, catching, lateraling, and pitching actions using a milk jug.

BOTTLECAP GOLF

Players design holes for a miniature golf course using a variety of objects, including items that normally might be thrown out. Once the holes are laid out and a decision is made as to how the hole must be played, participants thump bottlecaps using their fingers in place of traditional golf equipment. Strategy is enhanced by a rule that allows a person to get a free stroke if his cap contacts another person's cap.

Objectives

Development of fine motor skills and the reinforcement of many golf rules and much of the terminology associated with traditional golf. Enhance students' creativity as they must plan, design, lay out, and determine exactly how each hole must be played.

Equipment

One bottlecap for each player. The twist-off kind that has a fluted edge found on brands of bottled beer and soda works best. Steel wool may be used to remove the brand name, and caps should be washed thoroughly. A small amount of four different colors of clay is needed for weighting, to prevent caps from rolling, and to distinguish each player's piece. There is no set requirement for materials to be used to construct the holes. Generally, the easiest approach is to bring out a wide assortment of items including jump ropes, cones, polyspots, tennis ball cans, small boxes, scooters, tennis balls, small pieces of wood, cardboard that can be folded to set up in placard fashion, the support material from empty rolls of tape, empty plastic cups, and so on. For each three to four players, provide a list of possible equipment to be used for the construction of the holes, along with two sheets of paper and a pencil. Each player records her score for each hole on an index card.

Playing Area

A relatively smooth surface is necessary to permit the caps to slide; thus, this activity can be played on surfaces made of concrete, blacktop, linoleum, marble, or wood. The typical hole requires an area of approximately 7 feet (2.1 meters) by 15 to 20 feet (4.6 to 6.1 meters) with at least 5 feet (1.5 meters) left between the end of one hole and the beginning of the next, and the same amount of space left on each side to permit players to move around for their shots. If space is at a premium, it is possible to design holes so that participants have to go around an object at the far end of the hole and play back to the cup that is located near where the tee shots were taken.

Participants

Three to four players can be accommodated at each hole.

Game

Divide players into groups of three or four, and provide a list of items that you have available to construct the course. You may need to place a restriction on how many of the same items may be used at one hole. Inform participants of the approximate size of the area in which they must set up all their equipment. Each group plans its hole and sketches or labels the obstacles along with hazards, traps, and so on, as well as their relative positions on a sheet of paper. The "tee area" and "cup" should be clearly labeled, as well as the path that must be traversed around and/or through the hazards. Short written instructions, or arrows showing the line of play, can aid the diagram. Each group collects the equipment it needs and sets up the hole in the area assigned. Once the holes are completed, the supervisor tells each group the number of its hole, which is then placed on the diagram. Figure 4.1 provides a diagram of a representative hole.

Players arbitrarily decide on a tee-off order for their hole, and play proceeds using the basic rules of golf except that the order for shooting is maintained regardless of where each cap is located in relation to other caps or the cup. Two additional regulations are imposed. A player is entitled to a free shot, which is not counted in his score, each time his cap contacts another cap. On this contact, if an opponent's cap is propelled, say, into a water hazard, a standard one-stroke penalty is applied to the score of the player whose cap landed in the water. When that individual plays her next shot, the cap is placed a few inches from the point where it entered the water. After each participant holes out, those players proceed to the next hole, while those completing the last hole move to hole #1.

Helpful Hints

Provide a diagrammatic example of a hole that has been constructed so that individuals have a good idea of the range of possibilities. However, it's best to encourage them to devise their own portion of "Augusta"

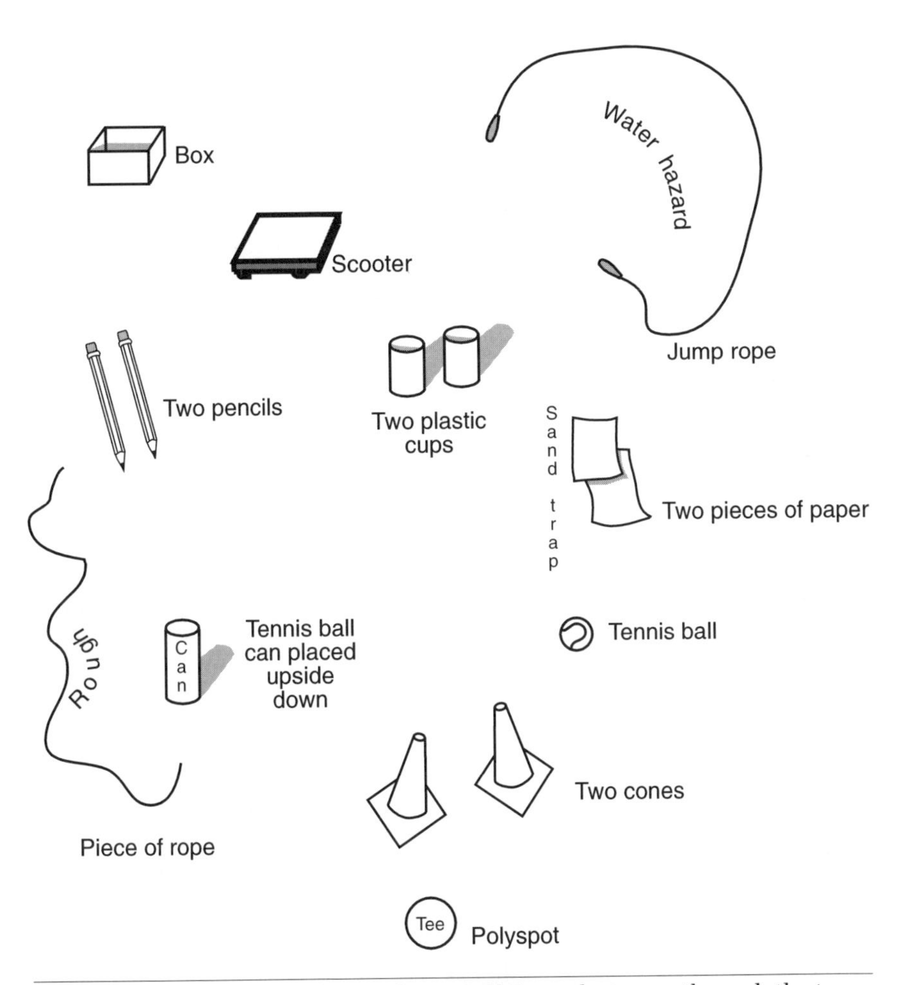

Figure 4.1 A sample hole for Bottlecap Golf. From the tee, go through the two cones, between the tennis ball and sand trap, then through the plastic cups to the scooter such that the cap is sent under the scooter from left to right, go around the box, through the pencils, and hole out by hitting the tennis can.

without creating something that is so obtuse that the time needed for setup or figuring out the requirements of play is excessive. Often it is best to take the last 10 to 12 minutes of a class period to plan the hole and draw the diagram, then at the next class allow five minutes for construction and the remainder for play. A hazard should not have a raised lip that completely surrounds its edge, for caps will rarely jump the obstruction. A fast way to create a hazard is to use a jump rope, positioning the open side of the hazard facing the direction in which the caps will be thumped. If this confuses participants, especially younger ones, then adopt a rule providing that if a cap comes in contact with the outside border of any hazard, the action is considered to have landed that player's cap in the hazard.

VOLLEY-TENNIS BROOM BALL

Players are required to use a broom to propel a volleyball over a tennis-height net from either a single bounce or on the volley.

Objectives

Develops striking skills, eye-hand coordination, and team cooperation.

Equipment

For each court, one volleyball and eight corn brooms with wooden shafts cut to approximately three to four feet (0.9 to 1.2 meters) in length. A hole should be drilled in the end of each handle and a leather or rope thong inserted. Fourteen marking spots for play on a volleyball court. When playing on a tennis court, use chalk or marking spots for the additional lines. Figure 4.2 shows the setup for a volleyball court, while figure 4.3 depicts the tennis court layout.

Playing Area

A tennis court or a volleyball court where the net has been lowered to tennis height. For both tennis and volleyball court play, create a line six feet (1.8 meters) from, and parallel to, the net on each side designating a no-rally zone. On a volleyball court, use marking spots to define the serving line, which divides the front from the back of the court, and mark the left from the right portions of the playing area. On a tennis court, the service line and the centerline serve these functions.

Participants

Eight per court and one referee.

Game

Action proceeds as in traditional volleyball with the following exceptions: The ball must be contacted with the straw portion of the broom (figure 4.4). The serve is delivered at the service line from a self-drop using a lofting type of swing with contact made below the waist. The server is permitted two attempts in order to complete a legal serve where the ball travels with a height of at least six feet (1.8 meters) on a fly over the net and would bounce in the opponent's court between the no-rally zone line and the serving line should that team opt not to contact the ball on the volley. After the serve, play includes the doubles' alleys.

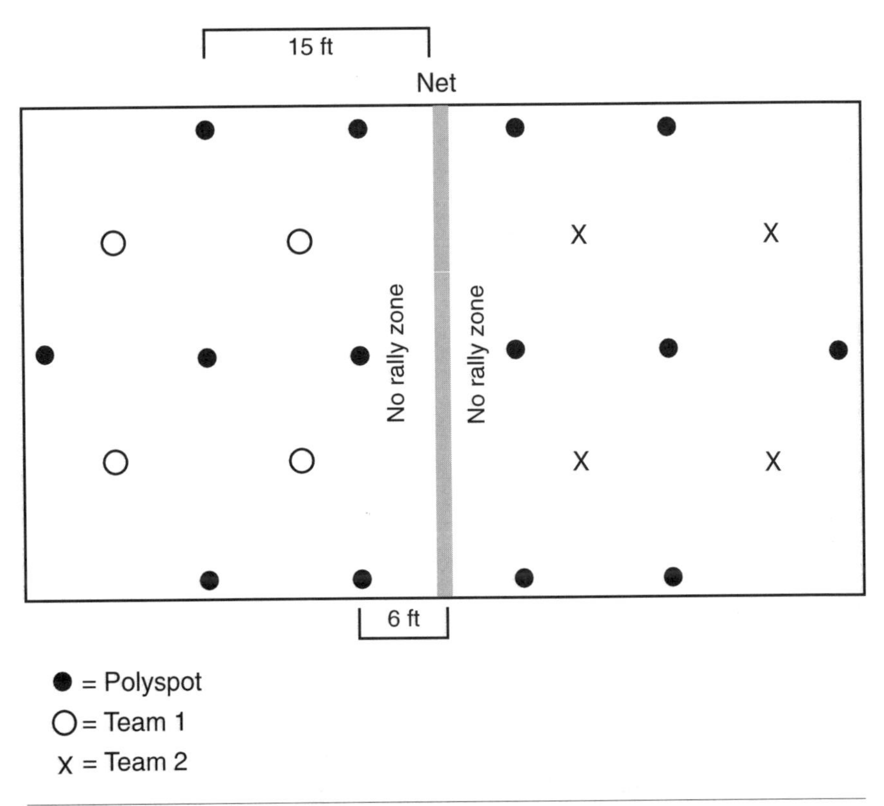

Figure 4.2 Volley-Tennis Broom Ball volleyball court design.

Violations

In addition to the standard rules of volleyball, a point or side-out occurs for the following violations:

- The ball bounces two or more times between hits.
- The ball rebounds from the surface on one side of the court over the net to the other side of the court instead of going directly over the net from a player's contact with the broom.
- On both attempts for the serve, one of the following problems occurs: contact is not below waist level, the ball does not reach a minimum height of six feet (1.8 meters), or the serve would not have landed within the forecourt between the no-rally line and the service line.
- A player's broom crosses the plane of the net, even on the follow-through.
- A player carries or lifts the ball with the broom, or contacts the ball with any part of the broom other than the bristles.

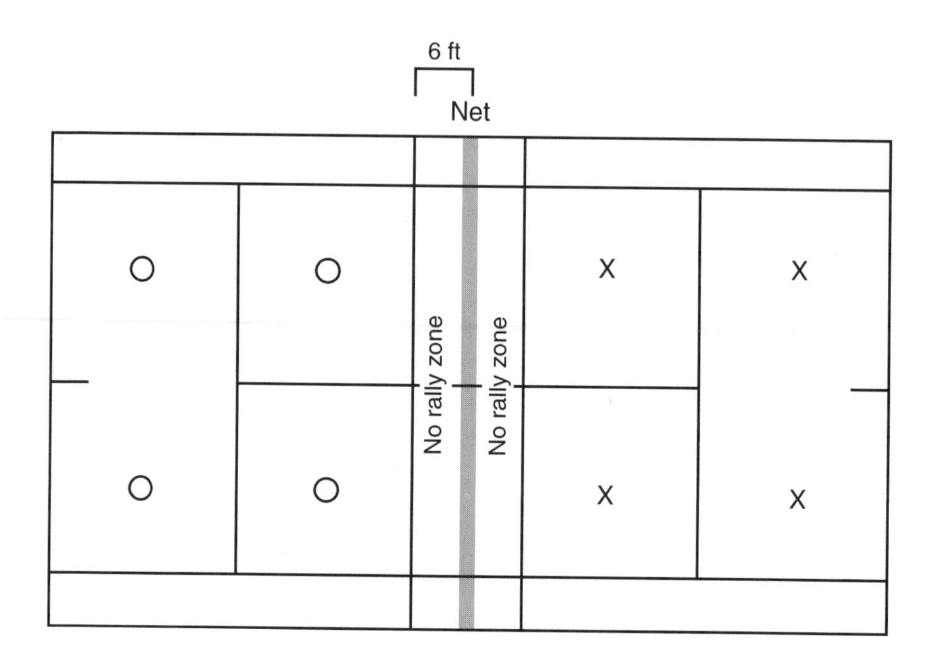

Figure 4.3 Tennis court layout for Volley-Tennis Broom Ball.

- A player sends the ball over the net while standing in the no-rally zone. Note, it is legal to play the ball back to one's teammates while the hitter is standing in that area.

Safety Considerations

It is vital that each player remain in his quarter of the court and call out if he will play the ball. Stress to players that they must keep a firm grip on their brooms and must have one of their hands through the thong. Emphasize that they can't play the ball over the net if they are standing in the no-rally zone.

Helpful Hints

Remind participants that the ball is still in play even though it might be beyond the sidelines or baseline when contact is made. This is paramount, for effective spike-like contacts are angled toward the sidelines, forcing opponents to move out-of-bounds for the return. Players should attempt to send the ball high enough to allow a teammate to get into

Figure 4.4 Volley-Tennis Broom Ball rally action.

good position for an effective return. The skills needed to contact the ball with the broom appear less complex than they are in reality. Accordingly, provide some practice time so players can get used to leaving adequate space between themselves and the ball. When waiting for the opposing team to return the ball, forecourt players generally position themselves near the sides of their quadrant, and two-thirds of the way back, while those covering the back court are located more toward the middle of their quarter of the court.

Adaptations for Younger Participants

Broom length should be based upon the age and size of the players. A shaft of two to three feet (0.6 to 0.9 meter) is suitable for grades five and six. Adjust the serving line as needed.

For third and fourth graders, whisk brooms with a tapered handle make effective choices. Because of the small lever length, use a beach ball and play on a badminton court with the net height at about four feet

(1.2 meters). The no-rally zone is located from the net to the short service line. Use marking spots, along with the centerline, to divide the court into quadrants. A line running parallel to the net and 11 feet (3.4 meters) into the court designates the area behind which the serve is delivered and into which the ball must travel for a serve to be considered good.

SHEETBALL BRIGADE

By passing and catching balls from sheet to sheet over an extended distance so that the ball finally can be caught in a trash can, players attempt to score as many points as possible within a set period of time or to reach a designated number of points.

Objectives

Enhances speed, eye-hand coordination, and teamwork.

Equipment

For each team, two to four twin-size bed sheets, four to six medium-size balls (utility, volleyball, soccer, foam balls, etc., totaling two more than the number of sheets), one or two 32- to 50-gallon (121.1- to 189.3-liter) trash cans, and four to six cones.

Playing Area

Any grassy or hardtop surface that is approximately 75 yards by 30 yards (68.6 by 27.4 meters) can accommodate three teams. Figure 4.5 shows the setup for two 30-player teams, each using three sheets. The first and second cones are separated by about 10 yards (9.1 meters). Cones two, three, four, and five are placed with 20 yards (18.3 meters) between each, and a sixth cone is positioned 10 yards (9.1 meters) from the fifth one. The three 20-yard (18.3-meter) intervals between cones two through five indicate the area in which each sheet group must remain while throwing or catching. The 10 yards (9.1 meters) between cones five and six serve as a buffer over which participants from sheet #3 must project the ball so the players holding the trash can(s) can attempt a catch. The short distance between the first two cones separates the two on-deck groups.

Participants

Each team should consist of 20 to 36 players, as a minimum of four players will be working as a group on a sheet. With teams of 30 or more, two trash cans should be used. One or two referees per team.

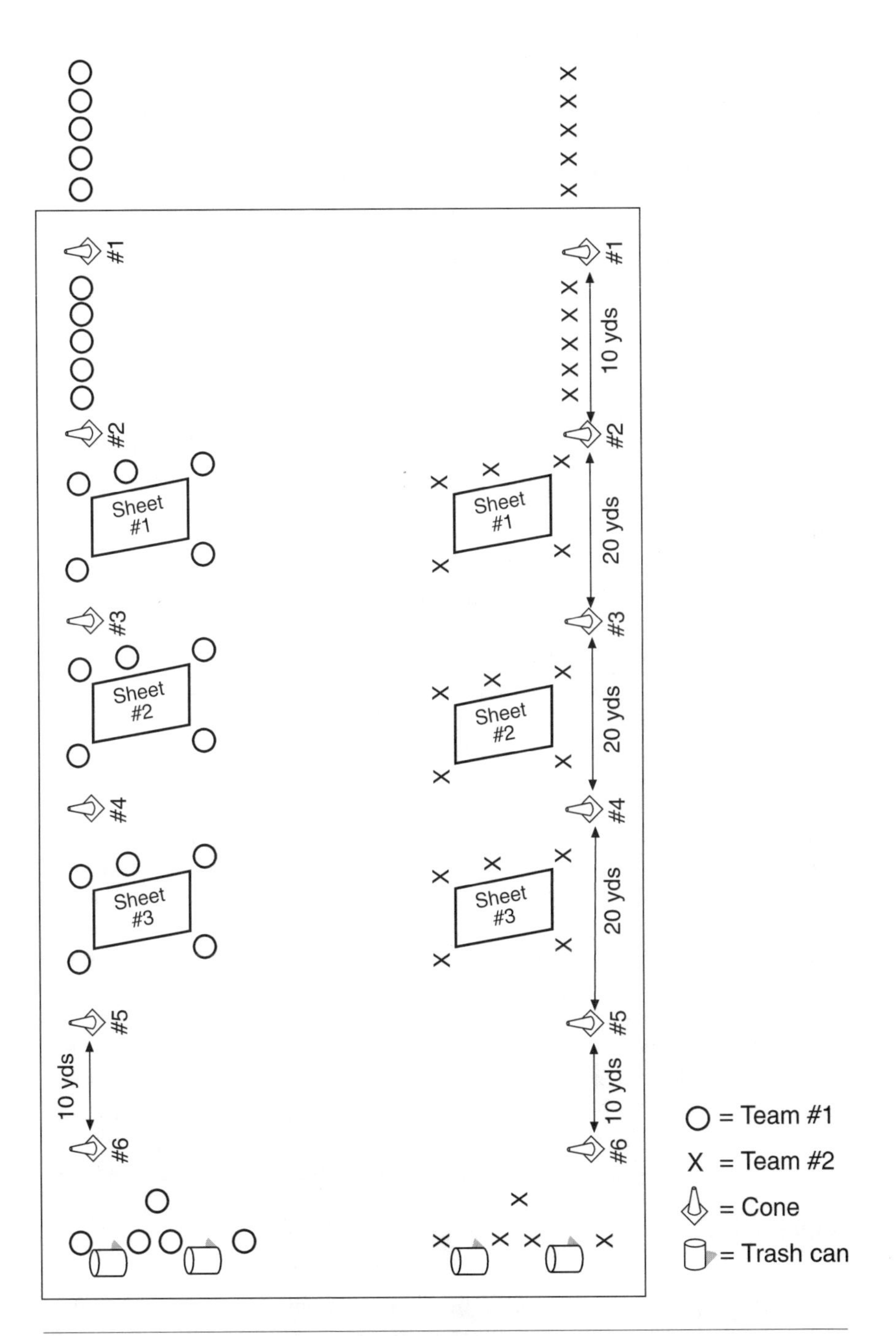

Figure 4.5 Sheetball Brigade field and player setup.

Game

Divide the class in half and then have each team count off by three more than the quantity of sheets used for one team. Thus, if three sheets are to be used, as in the following example, the class would count off by sixes. Note, it is not important if the number of players does not divide equally; however, each team must have a minimum of four players. Students are assigned to one of the following to begin the activity: on-deck group #2 (waits behind cone #1); on-deck group #1 (waits behind cone #2); sheet #1 (positioned between cones #2 and #3); sheet #2 (located between cones #3 and #4); sheet #3 (stationed between cones #4 and #5); or the trash cans (positioned beyond cone #6). Groups holding the sheets should minimally have one person at each corner. If there is a fifth person, that individual should stand on the side of the sheet facing the direction the ball will be projected (figure 4.6). Should a sixth person be assigned to a sheet, that individual would be on the side opposite the fifth person. The group assigned to the trash can should have two people holding onto a handle on each side of the can. Any others in that group will serve as shaggers. To begin the game, one ball is placed on each sheet and one ball is given to each of the on-deck groups. A total of five balls is used.

At the whistle, the players on the sheets throw their balls. The participants on sheet #1 toss their ball to sheet #2. The players on sheet #2 send their ball to sheet #3. The players on sheet #3 toss their ball high in the air so it can be caught by either pair of players holding the trash cans.

The teams stationed at sheets #2 and #3 and at the trash cans then catch the balls propelled to them. The players on sheets #2 and #3 must catch the ball sent to them from sheets #1 and #2 respectively. The players

Figure 4.6 Passing and catching actions in Sheetball Brigade.

stationed at the trash cans catch the ball propelled to them from sheet #3. Players on sheet #1 will not have a ball to catch.

The teams then rotate. Players on sheet #1 may move into position around sheet #2 immediately after throwing their ball since they do not have a ball to catch. Players on sheet #2 may move to sheet #3 after catching the ball propelled to them from sheet #1. Players on sheet #3 move to occupy the trash can station after catching the ball sent to them from sheet #2. After catching the ball from sheet #3, the players stationed at the trash cans bring the ball with them and run to replace on-deck group #2. Meanwhile, on-deck group #1 has now placed its ball on sheet #1 and is in position to project the ball to sheet #2. On-deck group #2 moves up with its ball in hand to become on-deck group #1. (Note, often players who move to the on-deck area from the trash cans will be the only on-deck group, as generally it takes more time to run from the cans to the on-deck area than it does for the initial two on-deck groups to move onto sheet #1.) Thus, a continuous circular changing of group positions occurs throughout this activity.

Points are scored according to the type of catch that is made. Five points are awarded for a ball that is caught on the fly, three points for a ball that is secured in the can after one bounce, and one point for a ball caught after bouncing twice.

Additional Rules

Violation of the following rules results in the team not being awarded points for that ball even if a successful catch is completed by the players on the trash cans:

- During play, the only time hands may be used to place a ball on a sheet is when the on-deck group initially places its ball on sheet #1. If a ball falls onto the ground, sheet players can use only their feet to reposition the ball so it may be thrown again.
- Each sheet group must throw and catch each ball in the proper sequence and can't project a ball that will skip one of the sheet teams.
- Sheet players must project the ball through the air and can't "pour" the ball from one sheet group to another.
- Sheet players must stay within their designated 20-yard (18.3-meter) space when projecting the ball to the next group or catching a ball sent to them.
- Each player holding a trash can must have at least one hand on the can during a successful catch for points to be earned.
- A player holding the trash can may not use any part of her body to catch the ball or redirect it into the can.

- A shagger may not physically assist players who are attempting to catch the ball.
- All catches by trash can holders must be made from beyond the last cone.

Safety Considerations

When two trash cans are used per team, encourage the pairs of players to spread out and call for the ball. Players moving from the trash can area to the on-deck area should run toward the outside of the teams, being sure to give the players with the sheets room enough to maneuver.

Helpful Hints

Be sure that players have had an opportunity to practice throwing and catching balls with sheets. Stress that high tosses are easier for the sheet and trash can groups to handle. Efficient strategy requires ascertaining that the group that is to receive the ball is prepared to do so and taking some extra time when needed to ensure an effective pass. Once one group is slowed, a domino effect results.

Adaptations for Younger Participants

With minor modifications, participants as young as fourth grade can enjoy Sheetball Brigade. Consider implementing the following changes: assign at least six to a sheet, or cut off one-quarter to one-third of the length of each sheet. Rather than having players move to the next station after projecting their ball and catching the next one, eliminate all on-deck teams and cone #1. Place all of the foam balls from each team by what was labeled as cone #2. At the whistle, the group from sheet #1 separately maneuvers each ball onto its sheet without using any hands and propels it to sheet #2. Once each ball has been tossed, the groups change, moving up one station. Those coming from the trash cans carry all of the balls, drop them by cone #2, become the members working on sheet #1, and continue this process until a set amount of time has elapsed or a set number of points has been earned.

TOWEL BALL PIN BOMBARDMENT

Bath towels are used to propel foam balls to pins or cylindrical targets. These objects are placed close enough to a wall so that they can be toppled by a direct hit, a rebound from the wall, or by a defender who is attempting to protect the targets.

Objectives

Develops agility, receipt and propulsion skills, and enhances partner cooperation.

Equipment

One bath towel, approximately 26 by 40 inches (0.7 by 1.0 meter) for every two players. (Players might find it easier for catching and throwing if a 1-inch (2.5-centimeter) hem is sewn down the short sides of each towel and a 1/2- to 3/4-inch (1.3- to 1.9-centimeter) dowel approximately 26 inches (0.7 meter) long is inserted. This will keep the towel from sagging if players are unable to apply the proper tension on the terrycloth.) One Indian club or cylindrical object, such as a tube in which shuttles are packed, for each participant. One foam soccer-sized ball for every two players to ensure continuous action. Eight cones to mark the boundaries of the areas in which the targets must be placed and two receptacles such as shopping bags or boxes to store toppled targets.

Playing Area

The game may be played indoors or outdoors, even if a wall is not on each end of the playing area. Any space from a volleyball court to a basketball court is acceptable, with larger spaces used for more highly skilled players. A centerline should divide the area in half and four cones should be placed on the playing surface so that they inscribe a rectangle of approximately 30 to 40 feet (9.1 to 12.2 meters) by 10 to 12 feet (3.0 to 3.7 meters). Most basketball courts are suitable for 28 participants.

Participants

Facility size dictates the number of players. Generally 20 to 28 may be active. One referee per court.

Game

Each player on two equally sized teams places a target within the coned area that each individual will defend. Encourage players to leave at least three feet (0.9 meter) between targets, or multiple knockdowns might occur. Players must defend all of their team's targets, not merely the ones they or their partners positioned. No elimination occurs, even if a pair's targets are knocked down.

To begin the activity, divide the balls evenly and have each twosome place a ball on the basketball endline of their portion of the playing area. Then have each pair, with their towel in hand, align themselves with one of these balls as each person touches the wall or is located at least five to six feet (1.5 to 1.8 meters) away (figure 4.7). At the whistle, players

Figure 4.7 Towel Ball Pin Bombardment simultaneous offensive and defensive action.

without using their hands (feet are acceptable) must secure the ball on their bath towel and run to the centerline, or another line closer to the opponents' targets, which players must stay behind when projecting balls. Should players cross that designated throwing line and topple one or more of the pins with a toss, no points are awarded and the targets are reset. Repeated violations are penalized by either removing one or more of the offending team's targets or by adding points to a team's total, whichever is more convenient. If a player uses his hands to defend the targets, one team warning is given before a pin is removed from that team or a penalty point assessed. Players may use their feet or towel to deflect balls, but care must be taken to avoid an inadvertent knockdown of another of the team's pins. An occasional violation for use of hands to secure the ball on the towel is generally not penalized; however, if it occurs excessively, penalize the offending team one or more points.

An inning consists of a maximum of three to four minutes or until all of the targets from one team have fallen. One point is awarded for each pin that is still standing, and the team with the highest total is the winner after six to eight innings are completed.

Safety Considerations

Fallen targets should be picked up immediately and placed in the team's box, not only as a safety consideration but because a pin that rolls could topple one that is upright and unintentionally penalize that team.

Helpful Hints

Encourage players to propel balls with enough force that they can rebound off the wall and topple targets from the rebound. Lofting shots are generally more difficult for a team to defend, as care must be taken to weave through their own team's targets to avoid knocking them down.

Occasionally, a team will purposely curtail the action by collecting and holding many of the balls. A 20-second rule may be imposed, forcing players to send balls within their control to the opposing team's territory in that time limit. Failure to do so results in eliminating one target from the offending team.

Do not attempt this activity without allowing sufficient time to practice throwing, securing, blocking, and, to a lesser extent, catching balls with the towel. The synchronization of partners' movements is the key. On the backswing the ball is somewhat cradled in the towel. As the foreswing takes place, just before the point of release, the tension on the cloth is increased by having each partner pull her corners of the towel toward her body with the towel at its full width as the arms move forward. This creates a slinging action. The angle of loft is determined by how high the partners' front hands are in relation to their back hands. The higher the back hands, the flatter the resulting trajectory. An especially important skill is for players to be able to propel the ball with a trajectory that is very close to the ground. To accomplish this, follow the instructions above and encourage players to bend at the waist.

MILK JUG FOOTBALL

Meld flag football elements with the requirement that players must catch a tennis ball in a milk jug, and an exciting version of a traditional game is created.

Objectives

Develops eye-hand coordination, enhances speed and agility, reinforces many of the rules and strategies used in flag football, requires a heightened awareness of other teammates executing laterals.

Equipment

One bottomless gallon milk jug and a flag football belt for each player. If flag belts do not easily distinguish one team's members from the other's, seven to eight pinnies are needed. One tennis ball. If play is to occur on a field that has no markings, 14 cones are required.

Playing Area

A grassy field approximately 30 to 35 yards (27.4 to 32.0 meters) by 70 yards (64.0 meters), where the actual length of the playing area is 50 yards (45.7 meters) and each end zone is 10 yards (9.1 meters). Cones are placed at the corners of the goal line and end zones, at the centerline where it intersects with each of the sidelines, and on each of the sidelines so each half of the field, exclusive of the end zones, is divided into equal portions. See figure 4.8 for a picture of this layout.

Participants

Each team consists of seven to eight players. Two referees are required.

Game

The flow of the game generally follows flag football, and any rule that transfers directly is not repeated here. A throw-off is used to begin the game and to begin play after each touchdown. Here the defense positions itself on or in back of the quarter line on its half of the field (the line between the centerline and their goal line), while the receiving team is located on or in back of its quarter line. No player from the throwing team is allowed to cross the quarter line before the ball is thrown. If the

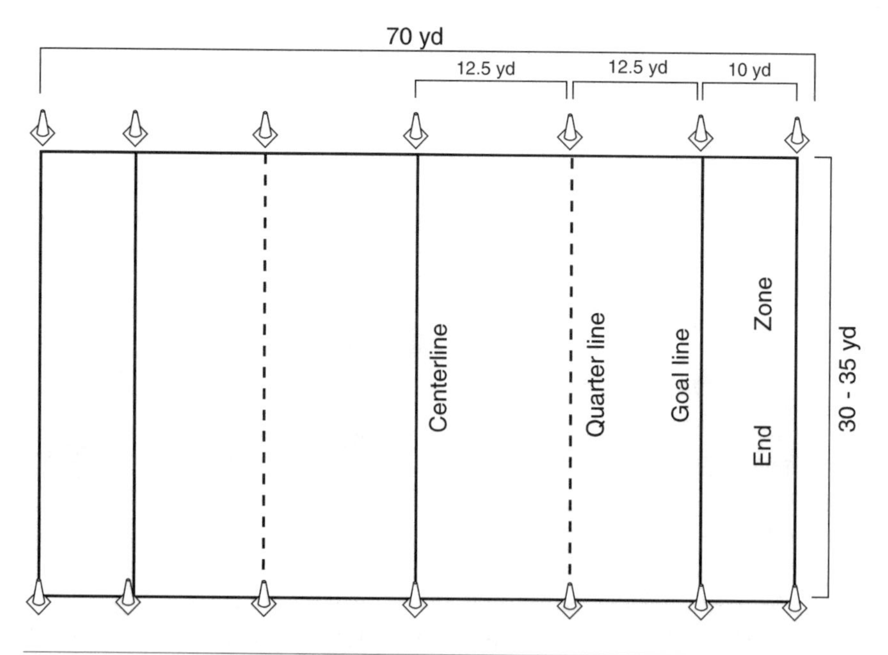

Figure 4.8 Field setup for Milk Jug Football.

ball lands out-of-bounds, the offense begins play at their quarter line or the line that is closest to where the ball went out. Action is stopped when the player who has the ball in his jug has one of his flags pulled or runs out-of-bounds; however, the ball is always hiked from a point on the field which is centered widthwise.

To start a play, the center must hike the ball to the quarterback (figure 4.9). A quarterback sneak is not permitted. As long as the quarterback does not cross the line of scrimmage, she may use either the jug or the free hand to catch or throw the ball. Should the quarterback advance beyond the line of scrimmage, she must play like all other participants and can't use the free hand to play the ball. Additionally, the quarterback is not permitted to place the ball in another member's jug (similar to a hand-off) with the free hand. Instead the quarterback must toss the ball into another player's jug using either her jug or her free hand, or a jug-to-jug transfer may be completed involving a "pouring" motion.

A team is given four downs to cross one of the quarter lines or the centerline. When a line has been crossed, a new set of downs results regardless of how close the next horizontal line is located. Defensive players may use only their jug hand to knock a ball away when it is in the air. Players may not use either hand to attempt to cause a fumble by knocking the ball out of an opponent's jug. Should a fumble occur, players are permitted to use their feet to either kick the ball to a teammate or to aid in scooping the ball into a jug, or use the sides of their jugs to hit the ball to another player or an open area.

Once the center has completed the hike, he may either stay in to block or may become an eligible receiver. In no case may there be more than two people from the offensive team protecting the quarterback on a play, or from the defensive team who will rush the quarterback after a five-second delay once the ball is hiked.

After a touchdown is scored, a two-point attempt is tried with the ball positioned five yards (4.6 meters) from the goal line. For the two-point

Figure 4.9 The start of a play in Milk Jug Football. Upon receiving the ball, the quarterback may lateral, pitch, or throw the ball to a teammate using either the free hand or the jug. Quarterback sneaks are not permitted.

conversion, the player receiving the hike is not eligible to run the ball across the goal line unless the ball was subsequently touched by another player.

Violations

Standard violations typically call for a five-yard (4.6-meter) or a 10-yard (9.1-meter) penalty, which is stepped off by the referee from the line of scrimmage. In cases where a player other than the quarterback uses her hands, assess a 10-yard (9.1-meter) penalty or half of the distance to the goal line, whichever is closer. Excessive contact or dangerous play should be penalized severely. Consider invoking any, or a combination, of the following penalties:

- Elimination of the individual for a certain number of plays.
- An automatic first down.
- Advancing or retreating to the next horizontal line, or if the flagrant play is on the defensive team when the offense is already positioned between the quarter line and the opposing team's goal line, use half the distance to the goal line or the spot where a two-point conversion would be taken, whichever is most advantageous.

Safety Considerations

As with any activity where incidental contact is bound to occur, referees should call the game closely enough to have a controlled play situation. Since the jugs are used to catch the ball, be sure that the cut edge on the bottom is smooth, as that portion of the plastic could brush against an opponent's hand or forearm. If rough edges are present, trim them or apply masking or electrical tape. Over time the plastic on the sides of the jugs may develop cracks, especially if the jugs are stepped upon or fallen on. Discard and replace these.

Helpful Hints

Each player must be able to toss or lateral the ball to either side of his body in order to allow the offense to continue to make progress when a player's flag is in danger of being removed. Prior to competition, have players practice drills in which they run down the field while spread out horizontally, with one runner trailing and another preparing to receive a pitch.

5

Discovering New Possibilities Through Altered Actions

Almost all physical activities require students to run or move without impediments and with unrestricted use of all senses. If you modify activities so players must use unfamiliar movement patterns or limited sensory input, you'll produce innovative games.

Games that require students to play three-legged or linked forward or backward demand partner cooperation and provide locomotor challenges. Scooters may be used in standard sport units such as basketball and soccer to produce other new possibilities. Players will have to modify use of their arms or hands if they are joined at the wrists, required to hold onto one another's waist, or joined hand to hand. When you limit or eliminate vision, players must rely upon other senses to provide them with the information they need. You may drape sheets across volleyball or badminton nets or require one person in a pair to be blindfolded.

A concomitant benefit of such activities could be greater sensitivity for individuals who are physically and/or perceptually challenged. Take advantage of such teachable moments by pointing out that some of these temporary limitations simulate challenges other people must contend with throughout their lives. However, because participants will not be familiar with these unfamiliar conditions, be certain to stress safety.

The Games

Activities played on scooters are presented first, followed by those requiring novel use of limbs and body parts. The last three creations are arranged according to the complexity of the motor skills required, with the final game being the most difficult.

SCOOTER SLALOM

Requiring individuals and pairs to negotiate a series of cones while using a variety of methods for propulsion creates a slalom event that at times parallels the version used in whitewater racing; however, participants are sitting atop scooters.

Objectives

Enhances upper body or abdominal muscular strength/endurance depending upon the exact action required (for individual and selected dual activities). Requires effective communication and teamwork for dual and group traversing.

Equipment

Eight scooters; 18 cones—nine of one color and nine of a second color; tape; nine five- by seven-inch (13- by 18-centimeter) index cards numbered 1 through 12, designating the order in which the gates are run; magic marker; eight lengths of clothesline or speed ropes measuring 9 to 10 feet (2.7 to 3.0 meters); 16 plungers; eight blindfolds; seven to eight stopwatches or watches with a second hand; seven to eight half-sheets of paper; seven to eight pencils.

Playing Area

A basketball court with cones set up to simulate a slalom course. Figure 5.1 shows two separate courses. Gates are set up so that a cone with a key color (white) must always remain on the participants' right when going through the cones. Those that are marked with an R are reverse gates, requiring the person to back through the cones. Note, if a gate is not marked with an R, and the key-colored cone is on the left as the person heads toward it, then it is an "upstream gate," meaning the participant must first pass the cones, then turn around and go through the pylons so that the key-colored cone remains on the right. In essence the participants will be moving against the imaginary current, or toward the location that they initially began the slalom course. Cones should be set approximately 24 to 28 inches (0.6 to 0.7 meter) apart so that participants must slow down to avoid hitting a gate.

Participants

A total of 28 to 32, including seven or eight judges/timers.

Game

Divide the class into teams of seven or eight. One team will run the course, while another serves as judges/timers. Note, two parallel courses may be set up on one basketball court. If this is done, two teams may traverse the course at once. Assign a judge/timer to one participant for solo events and two judges/timers for dual events. Participants traversing the course on scooters are started by the leader at 30-second intervals. Note, it is immaterial if the finish line is crossed with the participant facing upstream.

Scoring Possibilities

- Total Team Time—Add the times for each of the participants plus any penalties.
- Adjusted Total Team Time—Same as above except that the times of the slowest participant or the slowest and fastest participants are dropped.
- Places Based on the Fastest Individual Times—After adding any penalties, award points for the first eight places within the class. Note, if playing co-ed, you could award points for the best four males and best four females.
- Places Based on the Fastest Mixed and/or Same Sex Pair Times—Before the action begins, each team member selects a same- and/or opposite-sex teammate for scoring purposes only.

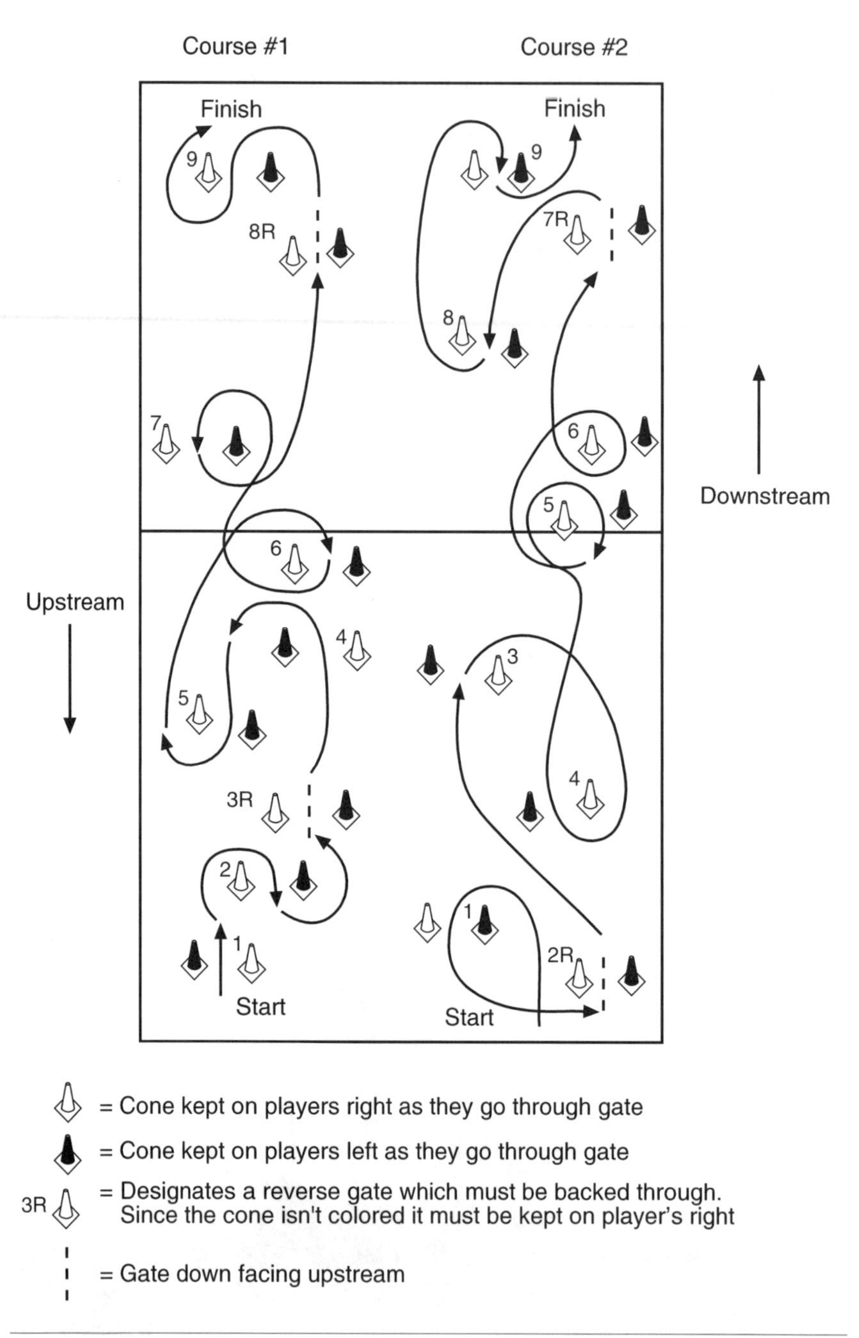

Figure 5.1 Two different Scooter Slalom courses positioned lengthwise on a basketball court. Arrows show the direction of travel.

In individual events these times plus any penalties are added together and points are awarded for places one through four.

Locomotor Possibilities

The following list is not meant to be exhaustive.

- Individual Run, Legs Only—each person from the team completes the course separately, and can't use his hands to assist.
- Individual Run, Arms Only—each person kneels or sits cross-legged, so that she can't use her legs to move through the course.
- Back-to-Back Run, Legs Only—two individuals are each seated on a scooter, with one facing forward and the other facing backward as seen in figure 5.2 with partners holding each other's hands. When traversing the gates, the decisions regarding violations are judged using the person who is facing forward (downstream); no penalty is assessed for the person in back, as it would be impossible for that individual to move through the gates correctly keeping the key-colored cone on his right.
- Individual Skier Run—same as the Individual, Arms Only Run, except that players are provided with two plungers. All action must come from the arms, using the rubberized part of the plunger for propulsion (figure 5.3).
- Back-to-Back Run, Arms Only—same as above, except that individuals must sit cross-legged and use only their hands to move themselves through the course.

Figure 5.2 Back-to-back slalom run traversing the second gate. The white cone must be kept on the right side of the first player through the cones.

Figure 5.3 Traversing an upstream gate during an individual plunger run.

- Back-to-Back Skier Run—same as the Back-to-Back, Arms Only Run, except that one pair of plungers is used for propulsion.
- Blind Pusher Run—the person on the scooter sits cross-legged or kneels but can't help to propel the scooter. A partner who is blindfolded must push the person on the scooter, who provides the directions through the course.
- Guided Individual Runs—a partner who walks the course verbally directs the person who is on the scooter and blindfolded how to traverse the course. Note, the following options exist: Legs Only, Arms Only, and Plunger Locomotion.
- Side-by-Side Runs—partners are on separate scooters both facing the same direction and with a piece of rope tied loosely around both waists or an arm circling the waist of one's partner; they may use both hands and feet. Other options include Side-by-Side Opposite-Facing, Side-by-Side Same-Facing Skier (only one plunger per person), and Side-by-Side Opposite-Facing Skier (only one plunger per person). For opposite-facing runs, correct gate traverse is judged only in relation to the first individual through the cones.

- Leash Run—tie the ends of each piece of rope together to form a circle about five feet (1.5 meters) long, or fold a speed rope in half. The person on the scooter grabs hold of a section of rope or the handles, while the walker holds the other end of the circle of rope. With no assistance from the person on the scooter, the walker must pull that individual through the course. Note, neither individual is permitted to choke up on the rope, and the person pulling may not touch the scooter.

If improper assistance is provided in any of the above runs, additional penalty seconds are assessed at the instructor's discretion.

Violations

Penalties are assessed for hitting a cone or passing through a gate in an incorrect direction, as specified below:

- Hitting the inside of a cone—add five seconds.
- Hitting the outside of a cone—add eight seconds.
- Part of a runner's body is outside of a cone when moving through a gate—add eight seconds. Note, plungers are considered extensions of participants' hands and to avoid a penalty must pass between the cones.
- Traversing a gate incorrectly—add 10 seconds.
- Missing a gate completely—add 15 seconds when sighted and 25 seconds when blindfolded. Note, once a gate has been missed, the participants may not retrace their line of travel and must continue with the next gate in sequence.

On a piece of paper, the five penalties should be listed so judges may record each time a given violation occurs in a run. Various options may be used to record scores. A combination of these enhances the excitement and teamwork.

Helpful Hints

Review the course with participants before traversing. Be sure plungers and the floor are completely dry or else it will be nearly impossible to break the suction while seated on a scooter. If the plunger continues to stick to the floor, carefully make three or four holes with an ice pick in the rubber by the widest part of the curved bell portion. If a cone is dislodged, the judge resets it immediately once the gate is traversed. To help judges know exactly where to reset the cone, place a small piece of tape underneath each cone when laying out the course.

Adaptations for Younger Participants

For players in the early elementary grades, the handle portion of the plunger might be a little long, but rather than trim off a few inches, have racers choke up as needed. Until children understand how the key-colored cones designate upstream from downstream gates, tape an arrow between the pair of cones to show the direction of travel.

SCOOTERIZED VOLLEYBALL

Volleyball gains a new twist when participants are required to move while on scooters (figure 5.4). Because of the reduced mobility, a smaller court space is used and the net is lowered.

Objectives

Reinforces volleyball skills and rules and enhances abdominal strength development.

Figure 5.4 A rally during Scooterized Volleyball.

Equipment

Two badminton standards, one net, two cones, one medium-sized beachball with a diameter of 14 to 18 inches (36 to 46 centimeters), and one scooter per person.

Playing Area

A badminton court, with the net at a height between four and five feet (1.2 and 1.5 meters). A cone, designating a service line, is placed 8 to 12 feet (2.4 to 3.7 meters) from the net and three feet (0.9 meter) outside of the doubles sideline.

Participants

Four to six players make up a team. Use a configuration for the front-back lines of two-two, three-two, or three-three, respectively.

Game

Action progresses with the same flow and rules of traditional volleyball with the following exceptions: The playing area consists of the entire badminton court, but if players have difficulty with coverage, the side and/or back alleys may be eliminated. Overhand serves are generally more effective, as strategy suggests that opponents should be forced to return the serve from deep in their court. A player's buttocks must be on his scooter for him to legally contact the ball; however, when a person is slightly out of position when attempting to hit the ball, slips off the scooter often occur. If contact is made prior to sliding off, play continues. Before that individual may play the ball again, repositioning on the scooter is required. Players are permitted to contact the ball with their feet. Inadvertent centerline violations occur because net players' legs extend beyond the scooter. These are not called unless the individual who is playing the ball gained a distinct advantage; however, net violations are watched closely.

Helpful Hints

Be sure scooters are lubricated so they roll easily. Encourage players who are in the back of the court to send the ball on a high trajectory to the front line. Remind participants that they may be located out-of-bounds while volleying the ball. Generally frontline players should be positioned fairly close to the net when opponents serve, leaving, in most cases, the backcourt players responsible for the initial contact after the ball comes over the net. Communication among competitors is vital to prevent a frontline player from misjudging a ball and rolling into the backcourt player who is in a better position.

Adaptations for Younger Participants

The net should be lowered so that most players while seated on scooters can reach to within six inches (15 centimeters) of the top of the net. The service line should be moved to within seven or eight feet (2.1 or 2.4 meters) of the net. If rallies are too short, add a one-bounce rule whereby the ball is permitted to hit the floor one time on a side prior to it being returned over the net.

BEACHBALL LOCOMOTION

Requiring pairs of people to transport a beachball between specific body parts leads to novel motor patterns that provide an amusing warm-up activity.

Objectives

Develops cooperation, communication, and novel motor actions.

Equipment

One beachball with a diameter of 12 to 24 inches (0.3 to 0.6 meters) for each pair of individuals. Note, if beachballs are not available, 12-inch (0.3-meter) diameter balloons or playground balls inflated to about 90 to 95 percent of capacity may be used.

Playing Area

Any indoor area where individuals may traverse at least 80 feet (24.4 meters) in a straight line. This activity can be conducted outdoors; however, if it is windy, balloons can not be used.

Participants

The number of participants who are active at the same time is based more upon actual space than the amount of equipment. An area the width of a basketball court will generally permit 20 to 24 people to move at once.

Game

Pairs of individuals place a beachball between specific body parts and, without holding onto one another or holding the ball, traverse a set distance. If the ball becomes dislodged, you may require that the team return to the starting line, another line that they had crossed, or stop and reposition the ball with or without the use of their hands. Application of the no-hands rule should be predicated upon the probability of successful repositioning. An asterisk denotes that repositioning may potentially be done without use of one's hands if the game is played with either a beachball or balloon. Repositioning without the use of hands is sometimes very challenging but can be made easier if a third person works with the two transporters. That third individual may kick the ball into the air, work the ball with the feet to the appropriate body parts, or press the ball between her elbows, permitting it to be secured properly by the other two individuals. Below are examples of some possible actions. Many of these can be varied further by requiring that students both face forward, both face sideways, face each other, or face away from each other while moving. Additional options could include having to traverse the distance by crawling, without the use of legs, or while seated on scooters.

Same Body Part Transport

Forehead to forehead* (figure 5.5)

Derriere to derriere (figure 5.6)

Shoulder to shoulder*

Chest to chest*

Hip to hip

Figure 5.5 Forehead-to-forehead transport in Beachball Locomotion.

Figure 5.6 Derriere-to-derriere transport in Beachball Locomotion.

Elbow to elbow*
Ankle to ankle*
Back to back
Thigh to thigh
Knees to knees
Back of head to back of head
Soles of feet to soles of feet*

Different Body Part Transport

Forehead to back*
Forehead to elbow*
Derriere to hip
Thigh to elbow*
Elbow to chest*
Hip to elbow
Forehead to shoulder*

Front of knee to back of knee

Back of head to forehead

Forehead to hip

The extent of the action may be lengthened by requiring that individuals complete a variety of options in one round. For example, forehead to forehead, elbow to shoulder, derriere to derriere, followed by forehead to hip. Each transport is done over the length of the playing area, and players may use their hands to reposition the beachball at the start of a new action. A second alternative is to continue the transport for a given length of time, say two minutes, and to count the number of successful trips to the nearest completed half-length. If scoring is desired, points may be awarded for the first five places.

Safety Considerations

Students sometimes have a tendency to veer off from a straight line during transport. The chance of injury is negligible, as players do not move that quickly. If a pair does interfere with another twosome, causing them to lose control of the beachball, they are permitted to use their hands to reposition the ball. If balloons are used, keep a few extras on hand should one break.

LIMB BOMBARDMENT

A novel twist is added to the traditional game of bombardment by eliminating use of a given limb that is hit by a foam ball. This leads to novel mobility patterns and greater teamwork and cooperation. Because scoring is based upon the number of body parts put "out of commission," participants are continuously involved in the action rather than having to watch most of the game from the sidelines.

Objectives

Develops bilateral throwing and kicking skills, agility, hopping, dodging, and crabwalk skills.

Equipment

Foam balls (varying sizes and shapes with an even number of each type of projectile) for one-half to two-thirds the number of participants. Using various balls reinforces different motor skills. A total of eight cones might be needed to mark the centerline and endlines if these do not already exist.

Playing Area

An unobstructed area of at least 40 by 80 feet (12.2 by 24.4 meters), divided into two equally sized spaces. A tennis court may be used for older participants, as the net provides a natural dividing line and also requires players to add height to their kicking action so the ball clears the net.

Participants

Twelve to 20 participants per team and one or two referees.

Game

Action is similar to traditional bombardment with the following exceptions: Initially, balls are divided evenly and are placed on the endlines, while participants are located at the centerline or touching the tennis court net. At the whistle, competitors secure the balls and attempt to hit opponents at the chest or below prior to the ball bouncing on the playing surface. Players may use a ball to knock another away and avoid being hit. If a player who is in bounds is hit on the chest or back or if a ball thrown by another is caught on a fly, the person who was contacted or the individual who threw the ball that was caught loses use of a limb of his own choosing—either a left or right arm or leg (figure 5.7). Note, this loss is for defensive as well as offensive purposes. Contacts or catches made while the player is beyond the side- or endlines do not count. Should the individual be hit on a given limb, then that body segment may no longer be used to assist the participant. When an arm is put "out of commission," the hand is placed in a pocket or in the player's waistband. If a

Figure 5.7 Limb Bombardment action showing players with various body segments that have been rendered unusable because they were hit with a foam ball.

leg can't be used, then players must use a hopping pattern or, if desired, a two-footed jumping action may be substituted, as one-legged transport can be quite tiring. When using this two-footed locomotor action, if the same leg is hit a second time, then the disabling condition automatically transfers to the other leg. Should both legs be rendered incapacitated, the player may either sit down or stand in a given spot and continue to throw balls provided at least one arm can be used. In the rare event that a player loses use of all four limbs in one inning, that individual may still assist her team by retrieving balls while seated or using a crabwalk pattern. A game consists of six to eight innings, each lasting three to four minutes. At the end of an inning, points are tallied with one point earned for each limb that has been rendered useless. In the case of a player who has lost the use of both arms and both legs, an extra two points is awarded to the opposing team. A player, other than one whose four limbs have been hit, who purposefully remains out-of-bounds for more than 30 seconds automatically loses use of a limb of her own choosing. Players standing outside their court are not permitted to throw at opponents.

Helpful Hints

Strategy generally suggests that loss of the non-preferred arm is less critical than the other free limbs. Players who have lost use of that limb may use that arm to deflect balls as long as that arm is not brought away from the body. Some protection may be offered by players who have lost use of both legs if they play directly in front of a person with full mobility, for they may shield balls thrown at that individual's lower limbs.

THREE-ARMED BASKETBALL

True cooperation must be developed when basketball players must perform all the required skills while linked together by a sleeve of cloth that players slide over their inside forearms. This positioning allows each player to use either hand, but both players must use identical movements with the joined limb.

Objectives

Stresses cooperation and communication among partners. Reinforces hook shots, which are executed less frequently in traditional basketball. A good change of pace where extra players can be accommodated.

Equipment

One foam volleyball or foam soccer-sized ball, 10 pinnies, 10 sleeves or tubes made of either cloth or elastic, and two hula hoops with diameters of 24 to 28 inches (0.6 to 0.7 meter). The cloth tubes may be made from a variety of throw-away materials, depending upon the size of participants' forearms. For narrow-diameter tubes, use large elastic over-the-calf athletic socks where the foot portion has been cut off just below the ankle (figure 5.8). The lower arm portion of a long sleeve cotton T-shirt, minus the cuff, will form tubes of various sizes depending on the size and style of the garment. If elastic is added to the top and bottom edge, shifting of the tube will be diminished. To fit two unusually wide forearms, portions from two sleeves can be sewn together. The tube is worn over the forearms, leaving the wrists and hands free.

Playing Area

A basketball court with a hula hoop hung over the back iron of each basket.

Participants

Three to five pair per team. One or two referees.

Game

With three or four pairs per team, full court action occurs. When five pairs are used, one pair each remains on the offensive and defensive half

Figure 5.8 Dribbling and defense in Three-Armed Basketball.

of the court, while the remaining partners play full court. Shots put through the hoop are each worth one point regardless of from where on the court they are taken. Baskets made from behind the arc are worth four points, rather than three. Elsewhere, shots through the iron are awarded two points, including free throws. During a free throw, only two pairs from each team are allowed to position themselves on the lane lines. Pairs from the team that fouled are positioned closest to the basket. In most cases, the rules of traditional basketball apply, and only those where obvious differences exist have been addressed here. Even though the foul clearly might have occurred to one person in the partnership, it transfers to both players, with each individual taking at least one free throw unless the offensive player successfully made the shot while being fouled. In that case, since only one shot is awarded, the individual who was fouled takes the free throw. All other violations carry over to each person in the pair, regardless of who really committed the error, except traveling, which applies only to the person who has control of the ball. A double-dribbling violation does not occur if the ball is transferred to the other person in the pair off a dribble; however, if one individual picks up his own dribble, the partner is not permitted to begin dribbling unless a player from a different pair touched the ball. After each quarter of five to eight minutes, players switch positions so that their opposite hand is free.

Helpful Hints

Encourage players to shoot at the hula hoop when they are located further from the basket while other pairs from the same team move toward the backboard to secure a rebound in case of a miss. The defense will have a great deal of difficulty contending with an offensive pair that has gotten behind them, for it is impossible for them to both turn inward at the same time, reducing their ability to block the shot. Thus, if the ball can be passed to a pair that has to cut toward the basket, relatively uncontested shots will result. Be sure to call three seconds in the lane for obvious violations. This will reduce the amount of crowding that occurs in the lane. Playing a 1-2-1 or 2-2 zone defense will diminish inadvertent contact. To keep a more continuous flow to the action, if a wall is located beyond each endline, consider extending the playing court to that natural boundary where balls landing over the endline are still in play.

Modifying Goals and Player Setup

You can change existing games by altering their objectives or goals. For example, permitting a team to score in two or more designated areas or by using two or more methods, with each awarded a different number of points, changes the action profoundly. You can also modify games by requiring participants to aim at unusual targets. When hula hoops, carpet squares, balloons, duck pins, or bowling pins take the place of nets, goals, and basketball hoops, games take on a different nature. Traditional sports require teams to score by propelling an object into an opponent's stationary goal. If players attempt to score points by sending projectiles toward a movable goal held by a member of the same team, nontraditional games evolve.

Modifying the configuration of players can also result in new games. Dodgeball, a traditional favorite, takes on a new character when four teams form a square and aim playground balls at a large cageball rather than at their opponents. Another version results when you require participants to wend their way through a maze of opponents and back to their team without being hit below the waist. Normally, racket activities are individual or partner sports, but when you move badminton onto a volleyball court with six players per side, a team sport emerges. You can use the same idea in table tennis. Instead of playing on a regulation surface, require teams of four to six players to hit a Ping-Pong ball over a badminton net that has been lowered so that the bottom edge is about hip level.

You can use this principle systematically by applying a series of questions to the activities found in most programs:

- What other means could players use for scoring points?
- Can a different type of target be employed in this game?
- What would be the result if the goal area or target were repositioned on the playing surface?
- How can the target or goal normally used in this game be made movable?
- What other boundary or court design could be used in this activity?
- How can players' positions be modified to alter the game?
- How can a team sport be modified to become an individual or dual activity? Even more important for large classes, how can an individual or dual sport be changed into a team game?

You can use this same sequence of questions to modify the innovative games that you develop using the other seven tenets identified in this book.

The Games

When considering the complexity of the motor actions required for success, note that the activities in this chapter are ordered along a difficulty continuum from the easiest to the most challenging.

RUNNING BASES

An excellent warm-up activity in which participants attempt to steal 12 bases before being tagged out a total of three times. Whichever occurs first, the runner then changes position with the baseman. A second variation has participants trying to steal as many bases as possible within a set amount of time.

Objectives

Develops speed, agility, throwing, catching, and stealing skills.

Equipment

One foam or regular tennis ball per set of bases, eight polyspots to define the two bases. The width of each base is as large as the base path. Generally the six-foot (1.8-meter) base width is judged rather than setting down definite marks. If played indoors, the side alleys of a badminton court may be used, with some enlargement for the base paths, and expanded areas at the intersection of the side and back alleys can serve as the bases.

Playing Area

Each pair of bases requires about 40 to 60 feet (12.2 to 18.3 meters) between them and a base path approximately six feet (1.8 meters) wide.

Participants

Four to six players per set of bases.

Game

From the players assigned to a set of bases, two become the basemen, and the others serve as runners divided as evenly as possible between the two bases to begin the game. Basemen usually play five feet (1.5 meters) in front of their bases. Any number of runners may occupy a base at the same time, but runners may not remain at a base more than 15 seconds. Once they leave a base, they may not return to it before touching the other base. If this rule is not followed, an out is given to that runner. The basemen toss the ball back and forth, attempting to tag runners as they pass by. Runners keep track of the number of bases successfully stolen and the number of outs they have accrued. All runners can potentially be moving at the same time so the action is very fast (figure 6.1). Once a runner receives an out, he should move out of the base path and walk to the base he was originally headed toward and continue to attempt to steal additional bases. Should a base runner be hit by a ball, no automatic steal or out is awarded. Play just continues.

Version One

Steal 12 bases before being tagged three times. Once the 12th base has been successfully stolen or a third out awarded to a runner, the runner and that baseman exchange places. Eventually everyone will get a chance to be a base runner and baseman one or more times.

Figure 6.1 Action of runners and basemen in Running Bases.

Version Two

Play proceeds for intervals of three to four minutes. The pair of basemen are a team working against all other base runners. Each base runner mentally keeps track of the number of his successful steals while each baseman tallies the number of outs he has accrued on the runners. At the end of the inning, outs are subtracted from steals, and the total number of steals is the score given to the pair of basemen. A new set of participants becomes basemen and play continues. After each team has had an opportunity to be basemen a total of two or three times, the team that allowed the fewest number of steals is judged the winner.

Safety Considerations

With four base runners moving at once, the playing field can get crowded, but the traffic pattern is eased somewhat because runners tend to stagger their starts, run on both the left and right sides of the base path, and generally follow the base runner who left before him. Remind players who are tagged to exit the base paths on the sides so that play can continue without interference. Once they reach the base, they should continue with the flow of the game.

Helpful Hints

The following are two strategies to lure the runners into stealing bases: faking a throw to the other baseman and purposely bobbling the ball on a catch. The baseman does this while really maintaining control so the ball can be seized very quickly. Strategically, the runners want to force the basemen to throw erratically. If a baseman must chase a ball, a runner can gain multiple stolen bases very quickly. Additionally, it is important not to have all of the runners wind up at the same base at the same time, not so much to avoid a crowding situation but because it is much easier for the basemen to create outs. When all the movement comes from a single direction, basemen can easily tag runners. Remind students that there are no force outs at the bases, so it is critical that a baseman play in front of her base.

BASKET HOOP BOMBARDMENT

Players attempt to score by hitting the backboard, putting the ball into a basketball goal, or sending the ball through a hoop hanging from the back iron. This is done by using a kicking action for selected balls and a throwing action for others, while trying to avoid being hit at or below the waist.

Objectives

Enhances throwing, kicking, dodging, agility, and speed.

Equipment

Seven foam soccer-sized balls (three each of two different colors and one of a third color) and two hula hoops, each of which hangs from the back iron.

Playing Area

A basketball court.

Participants

A total of 15 to 18 per court, with 5 to 6 per team. One team serves as referees.

Game

Two teams are each assigned a half of the court to defend. The seven balls are placed at the centerline, and players are touching the wall beyond their endline. At the sound of the whistle, players try to secure as many balls as possible. Before each ball may be used offensively, it must initially be brought back to the wall the players had been touching. The single ball of a different color is the only one that may be used to hit opposing team members at or below the waist. If this occurs, the player must exit the playing area at one of the back corners on her half and run around the entire basketball court twice, outside of its boundaries, before resuming play. Three balls of one color are designated for scoring points by kicking, while the other three balls are thrown at the goals. Scoring options are shown in table 6.1.

If a player is hit with a ball other than the one designated as the bombardment ball, no points are scored. The game is played in innings of four to five minutes. Players must stay on their half of the court. Referees should be assigned per team as follows: one to record all scoring from the kicked balls; one to record scoring from the thrown

Table 6.1

Scoring Options in Basket Hoop Bombardment

Area	Motor action	Points
Backboard	Kick	2
Backboard	Throw	1
Basketball goal	Kick	5
Basketball goal	Throw	3
Hula hoop	Kick	3
Hula hoop	Throw	2
Hit opponent on fly at waist or below	Throw	2
Opponent catches bombardment ball on fly	Catch	2

balls, except the hitting of opponents; and one to track and record scores from the bombardment ball, making certain that hit players complete their laps. If teams consist of five players, only use one referee to track the bombardment ball for both teams. Play consists of six innings, so that each team can face each other twice. Total points may be kept across innings, or the winner of an inning can be awarded one point.

Safety Considerations

Remind players that when they kick the ball to leave enough distance between themselves and other players to avoid contacting someone inadvertently.

Helpful Hints

Generally, individuals who are in the act of kicking or fielding are easier targets to be hit with the bombardment ball.

Adaptations for Younger Participants

Establish border lines closer to the goals by using cones or already existing lines. This will lead to an overlap area where both teams are permitted. If this is done, restrict the locations from which kicking is permissible by setting two circles of polyspots near each of these the dividing lines. See figure 6.2 for this court design. Refine the bombardment rule to permit only hits on the front side of a player who is positioned within one of the kicking areas.

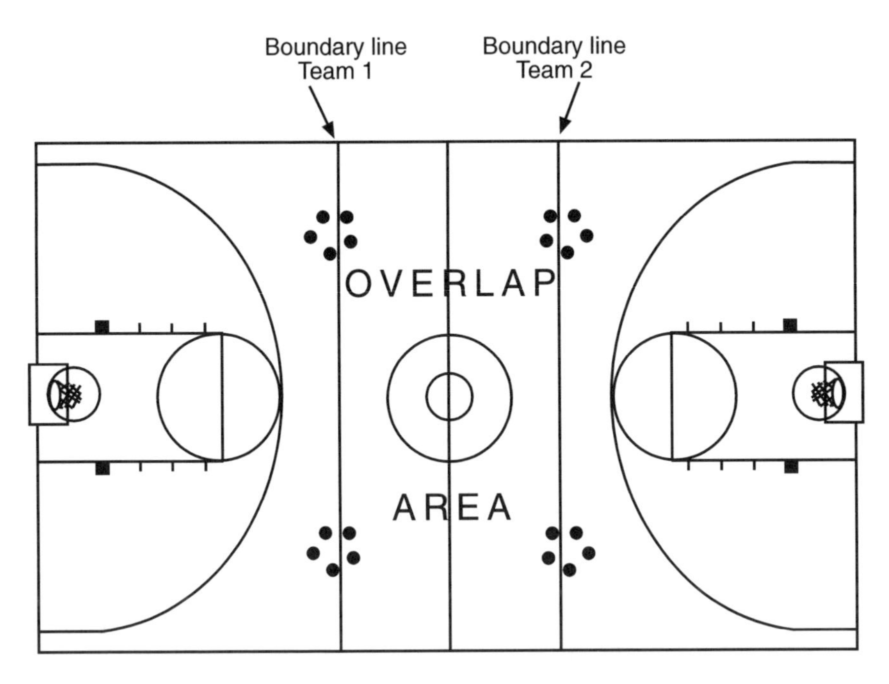

Figure 6.2 Modified court design for Basket Hoop Bombardment used for younger participants.

DOT BASEBALL AND BOX BASEBALL

Baseball is played in a restricted space by designating specific areas on a floor marked with polyspots or halves of file folders to represent offensive and defensive actions which occur in the traditional game. An opponent pitches the ball underhand into a box. The batter must contact the ball from a single bounce using an open hand. Where the ball lands dictates the result of that at-bat; no actual baserunning occurs.

Objectives

Develops bilateral eye-hand coordination, catching and striking skills, and reinforces general rules of baseball.

Equipment

Dot Baseball: for every court, 10 to 12 polyspots 9 to 12 inches (20 to 30 centimeters) in diameter or a like number of file folders cut in half with the tabs removed, one tennis ball, and tape. *Box Baseball:* for each court, six polyspots six inches (15 centimeters) in diameter or tape to define the corners of three contiguous boxes, and one tennis ball. Note, if either of these activities is played outdoors on a concrete or hardtop surface, chalk may be substituted for the polyspots and tape.

Playing Area

Dot Baseball: a court consists of an area approximately nine by seven feet (2.7 by 2.1 meters). Figure 6.3 shows a standard court layout; however, the exact locations and sizes of the polyspots may be altered depending on the players' skill levels. The logic of dot placement is to ensure that the possibility for greater offensive advancement is balanced by a

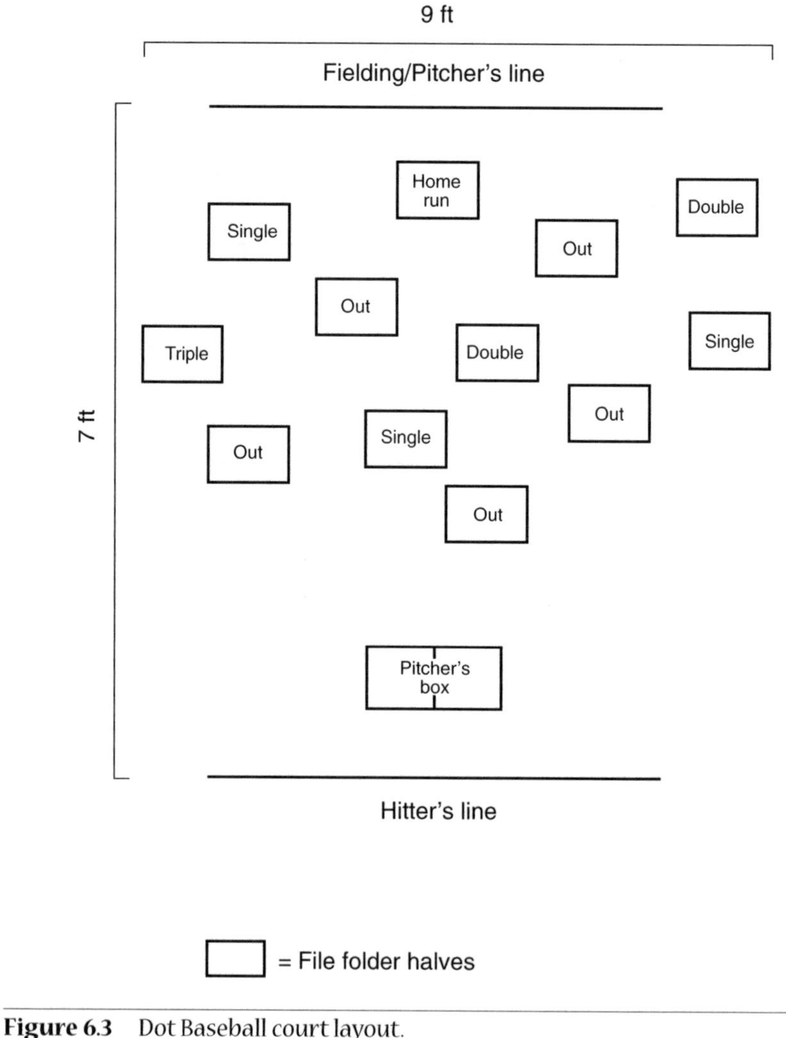

Figure 6.3 Dot Baseball court layout.

higher chance of defensive penalty. Four or five of the marked areas should designate an out. Box *Baseball:* three contiguous boxes, each approximately five by four feet (1.5 by 1.2 meters) as shown in figure 6.4.

Participants

Dot Baseball—two to four players per court; *Box Baseball*—two players per court.

Game

Dot Baseball: Player(s) from the field must be positioned behind the line farthest from the pitcher's box, while the batter is located in back of the line at the opposite end of the court. For a ball to be considered a strike, a defensive player, while standing behind the pitcher's line, must toss the ball underhanded so that it reaches a height of at least waist level and so that it initially bounces in the pitcher's box, an area measuring one by two feet (0.3 by 0.6 meter) that is two feet (0.6 meter) in front of, and centered with, the hitter's line. Any pitch that fails to meet those requirements results in a ball. The batter, without stepping into the court, must contact the ball, attempting to send it onto one of the polyspots or

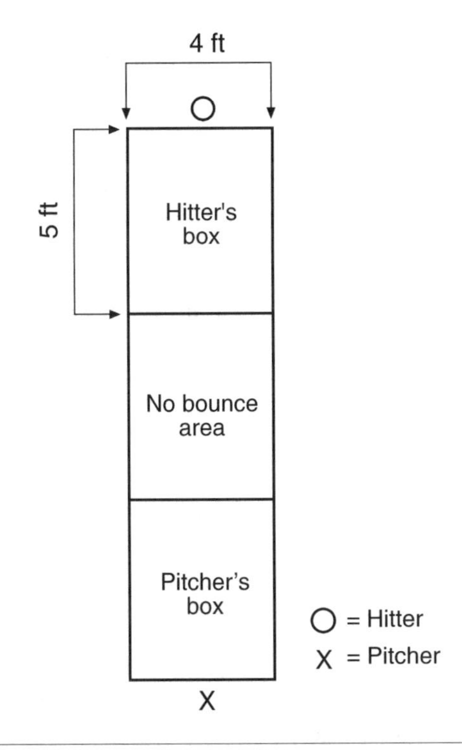

Figure 6.4 Box Baseball court design and player setup.

file folders. An imaginary runner will proceed around the bases. Should the batter contact the ball and it lands in the playing area, but not on a polyspot or file folder on its first bounce, a strike results. If the ball initially bounces outside the court, a foul ball is called. However, if a fielder can catch the ball on the fly without entering the court, the batter is out. With two players per side, alternate which participant serves as the batter after each out. Traditional rules regarding balls, strikes, outs, advancing of base runners, and so on, are applied.

Box Baseball: The pitcher stands behind an endline of one box, while the batter is located behind the endline on the opposite side of the boxes. The middle box serves as an area over which balls must be pitched and hit. Neither pitcher nor batter is allowed to step into the court.

For a ball to be considered a strike, the pitcher must toss the ball underhand with the same height requirements as in Dot Baseball, such that its first bounce must land in the box immediately in front of the hitter. If these requirements are not met, a ball is called. To avoid earning a strike, the batter must contact the ball with an open hand so that the first bounce after the contact is in the box immediately in front of the pitcher. Should the ball initially land outside of that box, a strike results. If the pitcher is able to catch the ball on a fly without stepping into the pitcher's box, an out occurs.

Imaginary base runners advance according to the number of bounces that occur before the pitcher can control the ball. After the initial bounce in the pitcher's box, the ball can rebound anywhere. If, for instance, the pitcher secures the ball after a single bounce in the pitcher's box, a single is awarded. Had there been any other fictitious runners on base, each would have moved up, regardless of whether there is a force-out or not. If a ball is in control after three bounces, a triple results. Should the batter step into his box while hitting the ball, an out results. The penalty for the pitcher stepping into the pitcher's box while trying to gain control of a ball that was hit is an automatic home run.

Helpful Hints

Before introducing either activity, be certain participants have a basic working knowledge of the game of baseball or softball. In either game, the pitcher should try to force the batter to contact with the hand that is least preferred. If faster play is desired, omit balls and strikes. For more advanced players in Box Baseball, substituting a racquetball for a tennis ball allows the pitcher to place spins on the ball. This is accomplished by depressing the ball with either a thumb or middle finger during the delivery of the pitch. By varying whether the ball is held palm up, palm down, or palm sideways, backspin, topspin, and sidespin are created, respectively.

Adaptations for Younger Participants

The concept of imaginary base runners is too abstract for most players up to and including the fifth grade. For grades four and five, provide a drawing of a baseball infield and four checkers that the hitter or her partner can use to represent the imaginary base runners. Also provide a pencil at each court to help players keep track of runs and outs. For second and third graders, Dot Baseball is far easier than Box Baseball, but reduce the scoring complexity by labeling the offensive hitting spots or folders with proportionate point values of one, two, and so on, rather than with a single or double, respectively. In Box Baseball, have each bounce count one point, where a maximum of four points could be earned from any given contact. Thus, points are tallied instead of runs. In Dot Baseball, if players' abilities are limited, add three or four more polyspots or file folder halves that reflect additional batting successes.

SOFT-VOLLEYBALL

After delivering an underhand serve, the player must traverse a set of bases that is positioned outside of a volleyball court before each opposing team player can pass the ball and return it across the net so it hits the court on the side from which it was served.

Objectives

Reinforces volleyball skills and emphasizes speed.

Equipment

One volleyball, two volleyball standards and a net, four indoor bases and one home plate.

Playing Area

A volleyball court with at least three to four feet (0.9 to 1.2 meters) of unobstructed space surrounding the court. See figure 6.5 for positioning of the bases.

Participants

Twelve per court with six per team and one referee.

Game

The defensive team is positioned in usual volleyball fashion. A serving order is established by the offensive team. While standing on home plate,

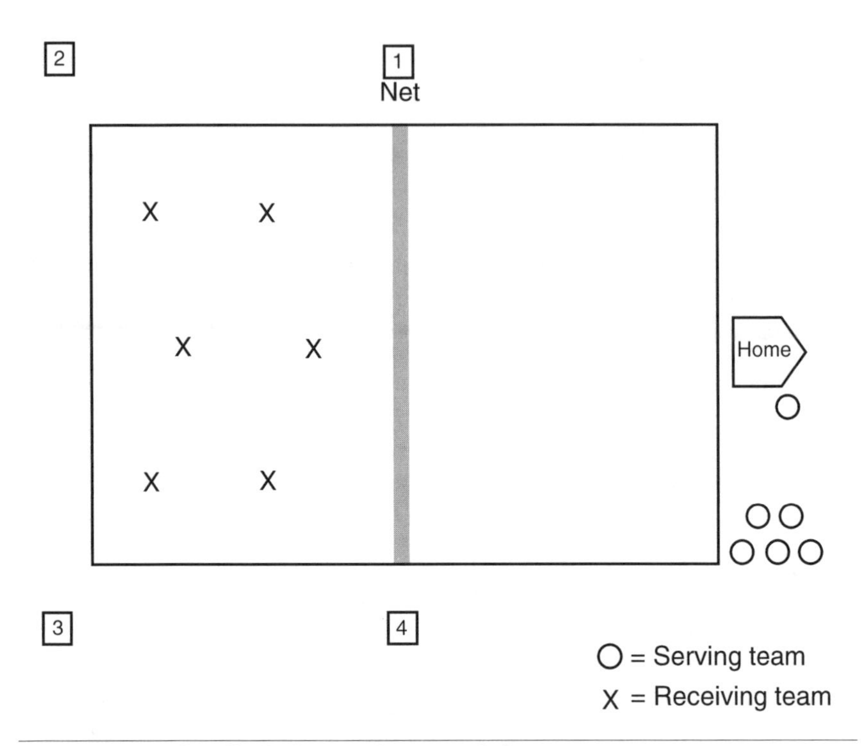

Figure 6.5 Soft-Volleyball court design and player setup.

the first person must send a legal serve across the net, then run the bases and return to home plate before each member of the defensive team in turn completes a pass and the ball is returned over the net and contacts the floor. If the server is successful, a run is scored; if not, an out occurs. A runner who purposely interferes with an individual volleying the ball is out. After each server, the defensive players rotate clockwise. Each half-inning consists of three outs.

Safety Considerations

Be sure to set the bases that are located near the standards far enough from the poles so that runners would not inadvertently collide with them. In the rare event that a pass forces a player into the base path, it is the runner's responsibility to avoid the passer. If this is not possible, have the player re-serve the ball.

Helpful Hints

Depending upon the skill of the players, various modifications may be added. If runners need to be slowed down, change the locomotor pattern needed to go from base to base. For example, skip to first, hop to second, and so on. If volleyball skills are weak, allow a maximum of one bounce on the half of the court when receiving the serve or passing. If the players are very skilled, consider allowing one player from the serving team to attempt to catch the ball once it is returned over the net, thus preventing it from hitting the ground and ensuring the run.

TENNIS BACKBOARD BASKETBALL

Traditional basketball takes on a new dimension when players are required to bank a soccer ball off a tennis backboard to allow the ball to rebound into a trash can.

Objectives

Reinforces most basketball skills, including shots that ricochet from the backboard.

Equipment

For each playing area, two coverless trash cans each with a round opening about 2 to 2.5 feet (0.6 to 0.8 meter) in diameter and height of approximately 4 feet (1.2 meters) and four cinder blocks or other objects that may be placed in the cans for stability. Should the cans lack sufficient height, cinder blocks may be placed under each. You will also need one soccer ball, six pinnies, and chalk.

Playing Area

A tennis court with backboards behind each baseline. The cans should be positioned in the middle of the backboard with the center of the can approximately 7 feet (2.1 meters) from the backboard. A square measuring 3 by 3 feet (0.9 by 0.9 meter) is chalked around each can, and a free throw line is set 8 feet (2.4 meters) away from the side of the chalked square that is nearest the net. Figure 6.6 shows the configuration of the playing area. Inbounds extends from the doubles sidelines to the backboards.

Participants

A total of 12 players per court with six per team. Two referees per court.

Game

Assign each team a basket, and specify three players from each team to initially serve in either an offensive or defensive capacity. Three are stationed at one basket and the other three stand at the other basket.

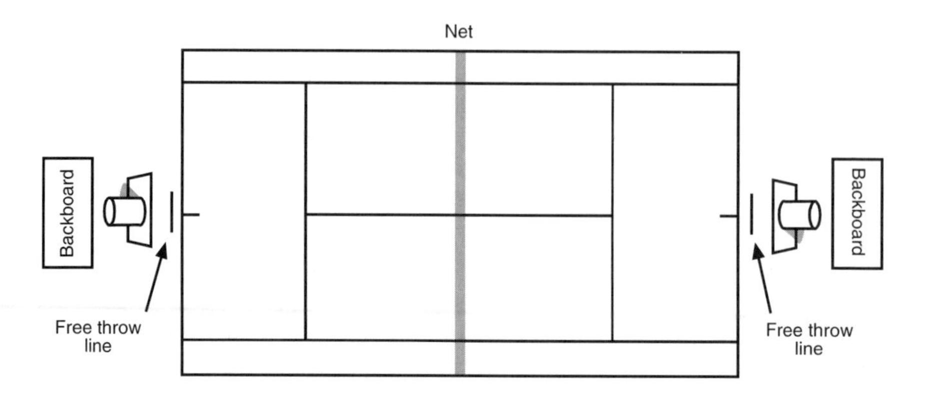

Figure 6.6 Court design for Tennis Backboard Basketball.

Participants do not cross the net barrier, playing only half the court until two baskets have been scored or five minutes of running time has elapsed. Each basket is worth one point regardless of whether it is made from the field or on a free throw. If a foul occurs in the act of shooting, only one free throw is awarded. A game consists of two 15-minute periods with a five-minute break between the halves.

A coin toss decides which team's defense will be given the ball at the junction of the service line and the centerline. All rules of traditional basketball apply, except as noted above and the requirement that a ball must rebound from the wall into the basket in order to score. Additionally, no player is permitted to touch the ball from the time it rebounds off a backboard until it bounces on the playing surface. Players may go behind the trash cans but may not enter into the square surrounding the can. Non-shooting transgressions are assessed at the spot where the problem occurred. Here the player has five seconds to make a pass, while the defender must play at least three feet away. After the five seconds, the defender can face guard the person with the ball. On a free throw, all players except the shooter are positioned behind the nearest baseline. The ball is dead after each shot, and the opposing team puts the ball in play from the hash mark on the baseline. Violations and penalties unique to this activity are listed below.

Additional Rules

The following penalties may be imposed for interfering with a ball rebounding from the backboard:

- For a violation by the offense, the defense takes the ball on the baseline hash mark.

- If the violation is called on the defense, goaltending occurs, and one point is awarded to the team that shot the ball.

Entry into the chalked area may bring the following penalties:

- For an offensive violation, the defense takes the ball on the baseline hash mark.
- For a defensive violation, one free throw is awarded.

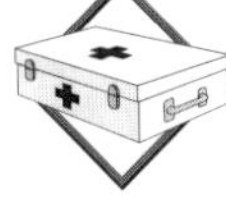

Safety Considerations

Penalize excessive bodily contact near the backboards by awarding free throws as needed. Remind players to stop their momentum well before the net. Should running into the net be a problem, plastic spots can be placed parallel to the net, about four feet (1.2 meters) away, to define a no-entry zone.

Helpful Hints

Players initially may not realize that to be successful they must bank the ball fairly high off the backboard and with a reasonable amount of force. This skill is not exceptionally easy to master, and games tend to be low scoring. To enhance scoring, consider making baskets worth three points, while a ball that hits the can directly on a rebound from the backboard is awarded one point. If such a scoring system is incorporated, have players change ends every time at least six points have been scored total and adjust the number of free throws accordingly.

PUNCHBALL IN THE ROUND

Players punch a ball into a no out-of-bounds baseball/softball configuration that possesses a double set of bases with a common home plate area. Base runners may choose to run either set of bases but must travel in the usual order, from first through home.

Objectives

Reinforces most skills and general rules of baseball/softball while enhancing baserunning strategy.

Equipment

One racquetball, two sets of bases, and two home plates. If pitching is used, two pitching rubbers. Chalk to mark the three- by two-foot (0.9- by 0.6-meter) pitchers' boxes, located three feet (0.9 meter) in front of each home plate, designating where the pitch should bounce, and the baserunning decision arrows positioned 20 feet (6.1 meters) from home plate in line with each of the first and third bases.

Playing Area

Any field that is free of obstructions and large enough to permit two sets of bases to be positioned with a common home plate area. The distance between bases will depend upon the players' skills, with 60 to 80 feet (18.3 to 24.4 meters) between the bags. Generally, the weaker the defensive ability relative to the players' abilities to punch the ball into the field, the farther apart the bases should be. Figure 6.7 shows the field layout and positioning of the defense.

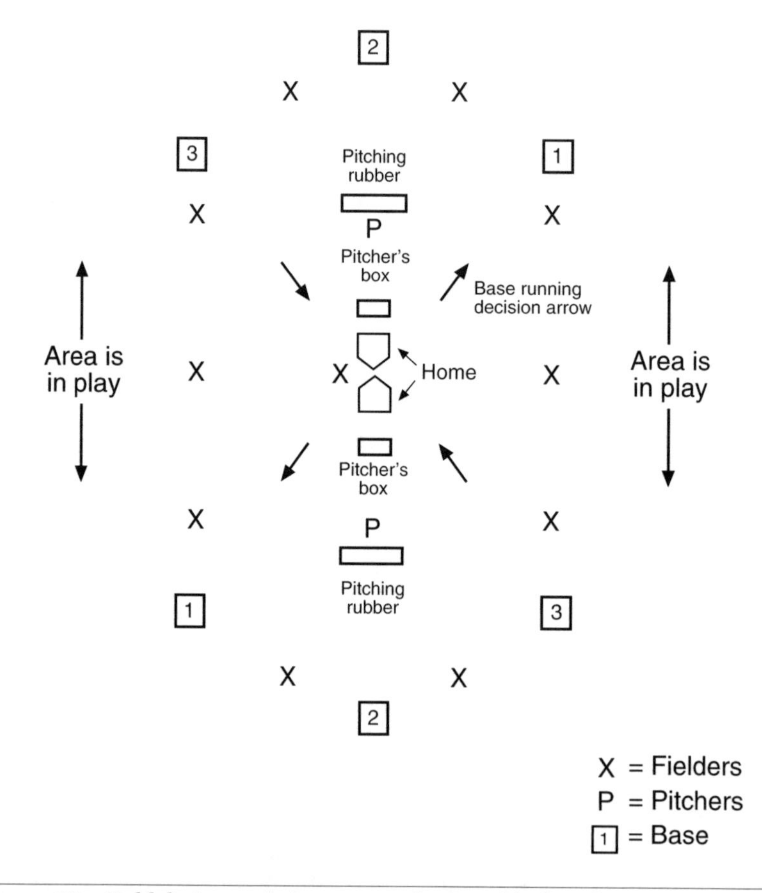

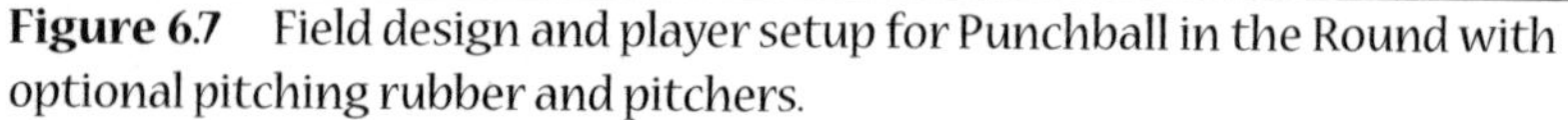

Figure 6.7 Field design and player setup for Punchball in the Round with optional pitching rubber and pitchers.

Participants

Twelve to 14 players per team and two or three umpires.

Game

Most of the rules of softball apply; only exceptions have been noted. The non-pitcher version of the activity involves punching the ball from either a self-toss or a self-drop. The pitcher version involves contacting a ball that has been thrown by another player. With less skilled players or when a faster game is desired, eliminate pitching. Regardless of which version is played, once the hitter contacts the ball with either a fist or open hand, he must decide which set of bases to run. Once the selection is made, he must proceed along that designated path, making certain that he completes his circuit of the bases in the traditional order, from first base through home. The runner is deemed to have made the choice when he passes any one of the baserunning decision arrows. If the puncher gets confused and crosses a third base decision arrow immediately after putting the ball into play, that base runner is out. If the runner starts down the wrong way but realizes it before passing a decision arrow, he must retrace the base path to home plate and then select a correct direction. When a pitcher is not used, the hitter may contact the ball after it rebounds from home plate or in the air from a self-toss. No matter on which side of home plate the hitter is standing, the ball may be sent in any direction with either hand since there is no area that is out of play.

When pitching is used, the ball must be delivered underhand with the same height requirements of slow-pitch softball. The pitcher is trying to have the ball bounce in the pitcher's box; however, if the batter chooses, he may punch a ball that fails to bounce in that area. If the ball doesn't land in the pitcher's box and the batter opts not to swing, the pitch is called a ball. Consecutive pitches need not be delivered by the same pitcher. In fact, one strategy is to try to catch the hitter off guard by quickly having the catcher send the ball to the other pitcher or having one pitcher throw the ball to the other, who will toss the ball before the batter can reposition himself.

In either variation, two strikes results in an out, and after two outs the fielding and punching teams change positions. Strikes are called when a puncher swings and misses, regardless of whether or not the pitch landed in the pitcher's box.

Safety Considerations

While it is possible for two people to arrive at home plate at the exact same instant, the probability is remote. This probability can be reduced if runners are instructed to cross the plate that is positioned closest to the set of bases that they have traversed, even though there is no real distinction between one home plate and the other for purposes of calling a player out or safe. A similar situation could occur if the puncher mistakenly runs toward third base when another runner is trying to get home. With the baserunning decision arrows and the sight of another person coming toward home plate, the chance of a collision is very small.

Helpful Hints

Strategy dictates that punchers direct the ball away from a runner who is being forced. The defense can often catch runners off guard by faking a throw from one field to another, having the catcher or another fielder cut off the throw, and quickly returning the ball to the player who is positioned at the base to which the runner is attempting to advance.

TEAM TENNIS-VOLLEY

This activity combines elements of volleyball and tennis. Three to four players make up a team. Players use a racket to hit a foam tennis ball over the net; opposing team players must return the ball before it has bounced more than twice on their half of the court, but a player must contact the ball between successive bounces.

Objectives

Reinforces selected tennis skills.

Equipment

Six to eight tennis, racquetball, pickleball, or Ping-Pong rackets; two to three foam tennis balls per court; one tennis net and poles.

Playing Area

A tennis court.

Participants

Six to eight players per court.

Game

One player is positioned on the right and left sides of the forecourt and backcourt. If a team has only three players, there will be only one backcourt player. A team does not have to be serving to gain points.

Since the action blends rules from both volleyball and tennis, key stipulations are listed below to eliminate confusion:

- The player in the half of the forecourt to which the serve is delivered must remain in the doubles sideline area until after the receiver contacts the ball after it bounces in the appropriate service court.
- The ball is only permitted to bounce a total of two times per side with a maximum of two players contacting the ball before it is sent to the opposing team. There must not be more than one bounce between one person's contact and the next.
- The same player may not contact a ball two times in a row.
- Volleys are permissible only during a rally.
- It is not permissible for the ball to rebound directly from one side of the court and go over the net to the other. Rather, the ball must be sent over the net directly from a racket contact.
- A player's service is considered complete when he has served into the left and right service areas while standing on the appropriate side of the hash mark on the baseline as required in tennis. Once a player's service is finished, the ball goes over to the opponents' side. Opposing players rotate one position clockwise, and a new server begins her service from the right side of the baseline hash mark. During a rally, when a team consists of four players, the server's responsibility is to defend the back right quadrant. With only three per side, the server must play the entire back court after the serve is delivered.
- No part of a player's body or racket may cross to the opposite side of the net.
- Fifteen points is a game provided that at least a two-point difference exists.

Safety Considerations

Stress that players must remain in their quarter of the court and that they should call for play on the ball. Generally, balls that are hit over the head of a frontcourt player will be taken by the backcourt player located on that same side.

Helpful Hints

High setups are easier to smash, even if taken off the bounce. If an opponent is preparing to smash, frontcourt players should try to move back into their quarter of the court and position themselves near the singles sideline, as smashes usually are initially played by those in the backcourt.

When attempting to intercept a ball from a smash, just try to make contact and keep the ball in play, relying upon a teammate to return the ball.

FRONTLINE SHIFT VOLLEYBALL

Traditional six-person volleyball takes on a new dimension. After the serve is returned, and following the third contact with the ball, players from the front row must shift to the back row, while players from the back line must run around the court to a waiting area near the opposing team's baseline, as the three people who had been in the holding area move to become the members of the front line. Rotation occurs while the ball is in play.

Objectives

Reinforces traditional volleyball skills while providing for greater physical activity through interval-type sprinting.

Equipment

One volleyball, one volleyball net, two polyspots, four mini cones to prevent players from cutting across the corners of the court, and two standards per court.

Playing Area

A volleyball court.

Participants

A total of 18 individuals per court plus one referee.

Game

All rules of traditional volleyball are followed except as noted. Three of the nine players per team begin the game in a holding area located even with the opponents' baseline and about 4 feet (1.2 meters) from the left sideline when facing the net. Players line up behind a plastic marking spot. During a rally (after the return of the serve is completed), when the third person to contact the ball sends the ball over the net, the team must shift in the following manner: The front line moves directly back to become the back line; backline players, without changing their order, must run around the court clockwise to their team's holding area. The three people who were located in their team's holding area position themselves to play the front line. This means that the right front becomes the server; the person who had served last will be the end, or third person in the holding area; and the last person in the holding area will assume the front right position. See figure 6.8 for a schematic representing the shifting positions.

The serving team first rotates positions *after* having played the ball from the receiving team. So that each person gets a chance to play in each of the nine positions, after a side-out occurs, the following player movement occurs for the team that will be serving: The left back rotates to become the last person in the holding area line; the first person in the holding area line becomes the left front; and the other five court players rotate in the traditional circular pattern. See figure 6.9 illustrating rotation after a side-out.

Players are not permitted to cut through any portion of the court when going to or from the holding areas and must run outside of the cones. Holding area players may not leave until the ball has crossed the net

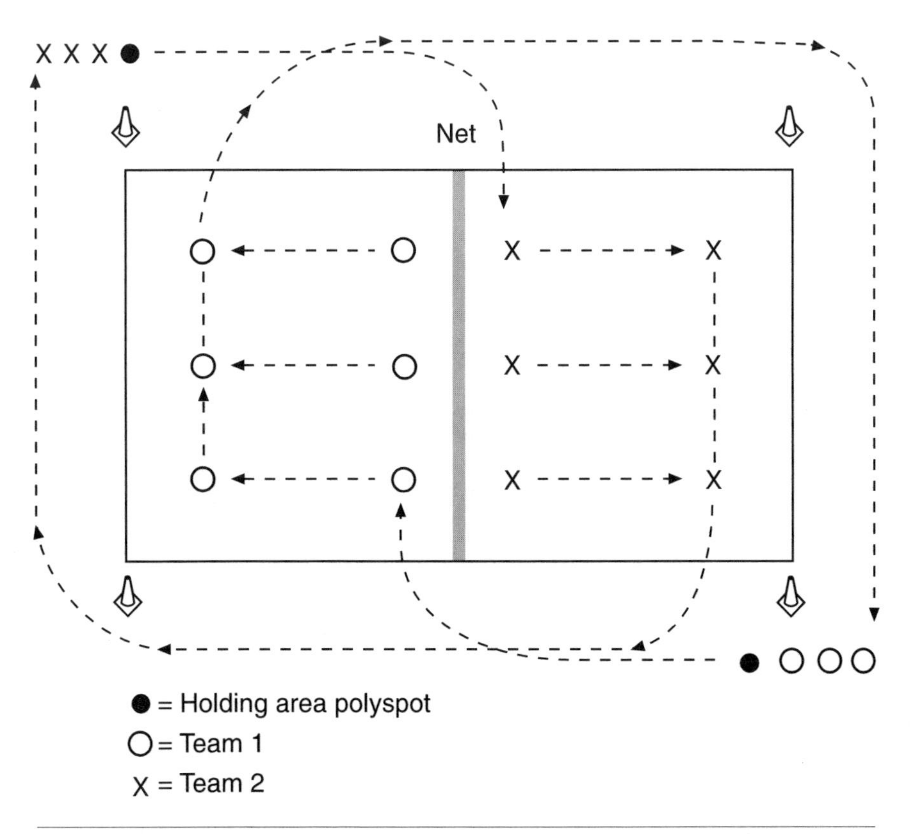

Figure 6.8 Shifting patterns during a rally for both teams when playing Front-Line Shift Volleyball.

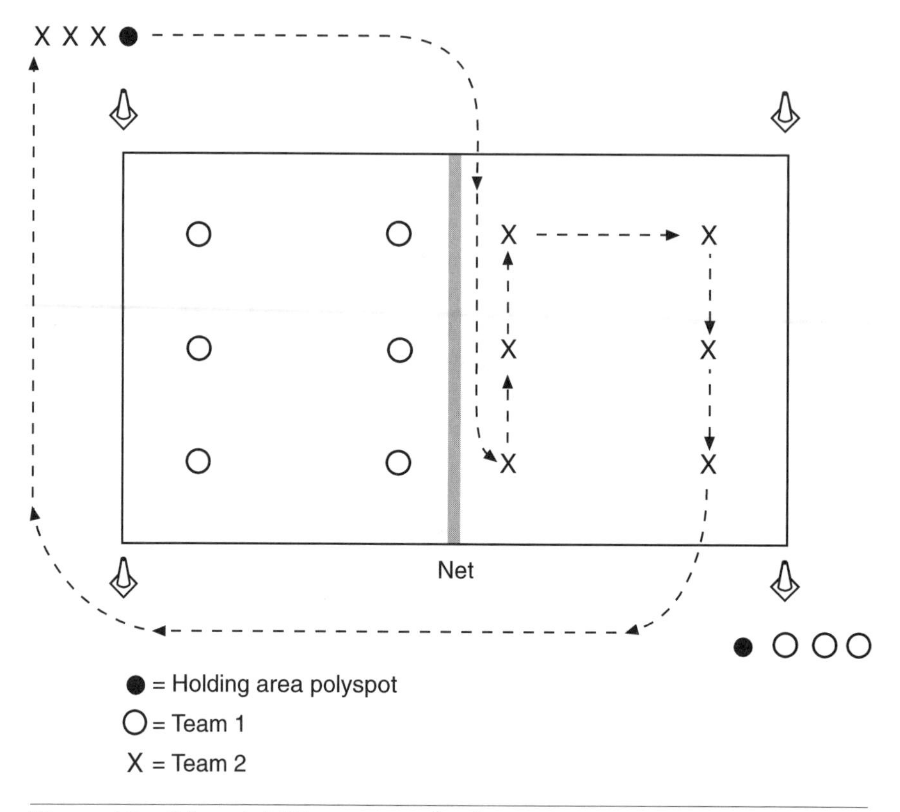

Figure 6.9 Side-out shifting pattern for the serving team.

from their team's third contact. If a player leaves too soon, a side-out or point is awarded to the opposing team. If a ball is played by a participant who should not be on the court at that time, a side-out or point is awarded. Should an offcourt player interfere with the play of the opposing team's court players, a side-out or point results. If during a rally (after the serve has been returned) the ball is sent over the net with fewer than three contacts, a side-out or point occurs. A player from the back line who mistakenly exits the court to shift positions before the ball has crossed the net may not re-enter his team's court but must proceed to the holding area. The penalty for improperly returning to the court is a side-out or point.

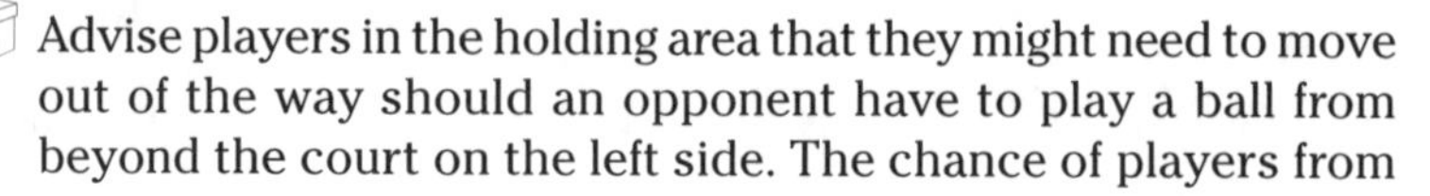

Safety Considerations

Advise players in the holding area that they might need to move out of the way should an opponent have to play a ball from beyond the court on the left side. The chance of players from teams running into each other is almost nil provided that shifting patterns are closely followed. Walk through the shifting and rotational patterns until players are familiar with the clockwise flow.

Helpful Hints

Strategy dictates that players during a rally attempt to return the ball to a location where a frontline player would be required to play the ball or to send the ball directly into the backcourt to try to catch the line before it can complete its shift. Teams should strive for swift passing to force one of the three moving groups to be in transition before the new front line is ready. If a team needs more time to reposition, the players should use higher sets. Obviously, the more time one team takes to return the ball, the more opportunity the defense has had to reorganize itself. Do not attempt to play this version of Frontline Shift Volleyball unless the participants are skilled passers. Modifications for those possessing less proficiency are presented under Adaptations for Younger Participants.

To reduce the possibility of players leaving the holding area too soon, encourage the person who sends the ball over the net to yell “shift” or “over.”

Adaptations for Younger Participants

Play with a beachball or foam volleyball instead of a traditional volleyball. Serve from a point halfway between the net and baseline, and limit each team to two passes to send the ball to the opposing team during a rally. Another option is to use a volleyball but allow the ball to bounce no more than once on a side before it is returned to the opponent. If participants are still not able to sustain points of long enough duration, consider employing the shifting pattern shown in figure 6.10.

In this configuration, the frontline rotates to the backline. The backline leaves the left side of the court (when facing the net) and moves to the repositioned holding area. Those in the holding area assume the frontline responsibilites. Because of the shorter shifting distances, only require a minimum of two contacts before the ball is sent to the opposing team. After an opponent’s side-out, the serving team rotates. The first person in the holding area becomes the left front, the left front player moves to middle front, the middle front player moves to right front, and the right front player becomes the new server and moves to right back. The backline also rotates. The right back player moves to middle back, the middle back player moves to left back, the left back player becomes the last person in the holding area, and each of the other individuals in the holding area moves up one slot.

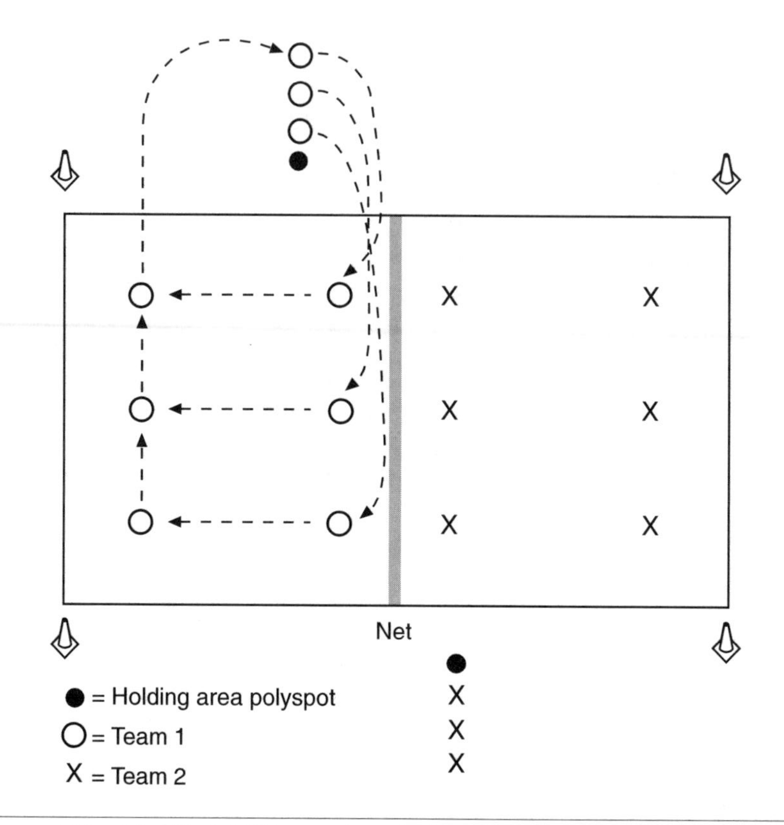

Figure 6.10 Modified shifting pattern for less skilled players.

Finding New Uses for Standard Equipment

We often see only one way to use a typical piece of sports equipment—the way it was originally introduced to us. But we can find new uses for standard equipment in two ways: by using it to create different movement patterns in an existing game or by using it in a different, but well-known, activity. Games that use equipment in a different activity may at first seem to represent a hybrid innovation. Further consideration will clarify the differences: If the new activity requires that similar movement patterns and strategies be executed while using a different implement, then the activity uses a standard piece of equipment in a unique setting.

However, should the game integrate rules and skills from two or more activities, the game could be logically classified as a hybrid.

Even though the distinction is not as clear-cut as some of the other principles we have discussed, don't be disturbed. The end result is still to increase the variety of activities for students. When you do so, you should have greater success motivating them, keeping their interest high, and piquing their curiosity. It's very satisfying when players end one activity session eager to find out what's on the agenda for the next one. Altering the use of typical equipment is one of the easiest principles for youngsters to apply, perhaps because they have less experience seeing an item employed in a set manner.

The Games

For the most part, the games in this chapter have been ordered along a motor skills difficulty continuum from easiest to most difficult in order for the games to progress smoothly and for the action to be competitive. However, Frisbee Skeet Bowling, the fourth activity, is the most demanding.

FRISBEE SOCCER

By requiring players to kick a Frisbee through an open-sided triangular goal, which is set in from the endline of a basketball court where natural boundaries are employed, a fast-paced game emerges that embodies a strategy similar to that of ice hockey.

Objectives

Enhances speed, agility, bilateral skills using the feet, and cardiorespiratory endurance.

Equipment

Six small cones, 16 polyspots, two Frisbees joined together at the flat surfaces by superglue or rivets, and six to seven pinnies.

Playing Area

An indoor basketball court, preferably with nearby sidewalls. Outdoor play is possible, but the Frisbee will tend to slide more slowly. An open equilateral triangular goal with 4.5- to 5-foot (1.4- to 1.5-meter) sides is surrounded by a circular no-entry area with a 6-foot (1.8-meter) diameter. The coned goal is positioned 18 to 20 feet (5.5 to 6.1 meters) from each endwall. A penalty line is positioned 12 feet (3.7 meters) from the diameter of the circle nearest the back of the goal. Figure 7.1 shows the court design and player setup.

Participants

Seven per team, with two offensive and two defensive players who do not cross half-court and three players who run full-court. One referee.

Game

Most of the rules of ice or floor hockey pertain with the exception of icing, checking, or undue roughness; however, incidental contact should be expected. Additionally, no player is permitted to cross the no-entry circle surrounding each goal. Thus, without goalies and with the goals positioned a distance away from the endlines, shooting may occur from 360 degrees around the coned area. A goal occurs when the Frisbee is kicked so that it passes through any two sides of the coned triangle at,

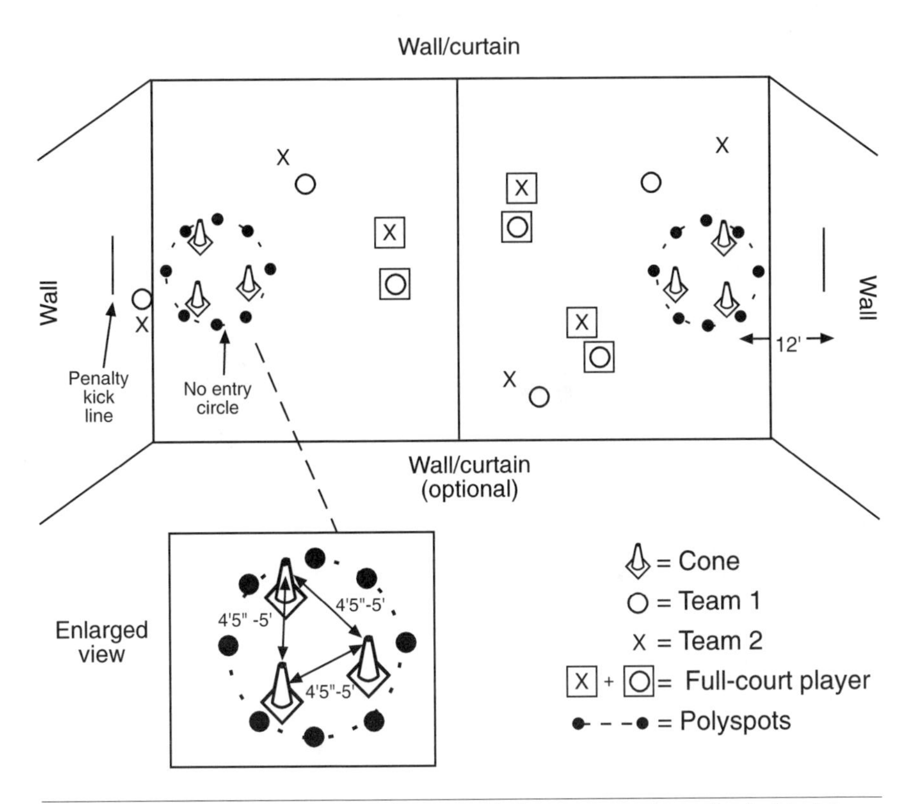

Figure 7.1 Frisbee Soccer court design and player setup. Note: play behind the triangular goal.

or below, knee level (figure 7.2). Only those rules that differ from ice or floor hockey are explained here.

Additional Rules

Violations of the following rules result in an indirect free pass by a member of the opposing team at the spot of the foul or on the no-entry circle, whichever is closer to the goal. During a free pass, all other players must remain at least five feet (1.5 meters) away for five seconds. Thereafter, players may move anywhere on the court except into the no-entry zones.

a. An offensive player steps into the no-entry area. (Do not call incidental transgressions unless the offense gains an advantage.)
b. A defensive player steps into the no-entry area but does not interfere with a shot on goal. (Do not call incidental transgressions unless the player interferes with the offense.)
c. A court player uses her hands to play the Frisbee.
d. A player obstructs the player in control of the Frisbee by moving between the Frisbee and the player who has possession of it. Players can avoid obstruction by playing opponents face to face.

Figure 7.2 Frisbee Soccer action.

e. Players fail to execute a penalty shot within five seconds.
f. A fouled player misses a penalty shot.
g. A Frisbee comes to rest within the no-entry area or goal.

A penalty shot is awarded to the opposing team when a defender steps into the no-entry zone and interferes with a shot on goal. During a penalty shot, all other players must be on the far side of the goal area.

Safety Considerations

Remind players to keep the follow-throughs to their kicks short to avoid inadvertently contacting the shins of another player.

Helpful Hints

Encourage offensive players to position themselves behind the goal to wait for a pass from a teammate. Remind players that the sidewalls are in play and that they may elude an opponent by sending the Frisbee to the wall, running around the opponent, and intercepting the Frisbee as it rebounds from the wall.

CONE SLIDE BOMBARDMENT

Players propel balls at cones trying to send them across a line located in the opposing team's court while preventing opponents from accomplishing the same goal on their half of the playing area.

Objectives

Develops kicking, dribbling, and throwing skills; reinforces agility.

Equipment

Ten to 12 cones, 10 to 12 foam soccer-sized balls, four tennis rackets, and four hula hoops. For younger players, use larger cones, but be sure they are light enough to slide along a wooden floor when struck with a foam ball.

Playing Area

A basketball court. Figure 7.3 shows the court layout and player setup.

Participants

Ten participants per team, one referee.

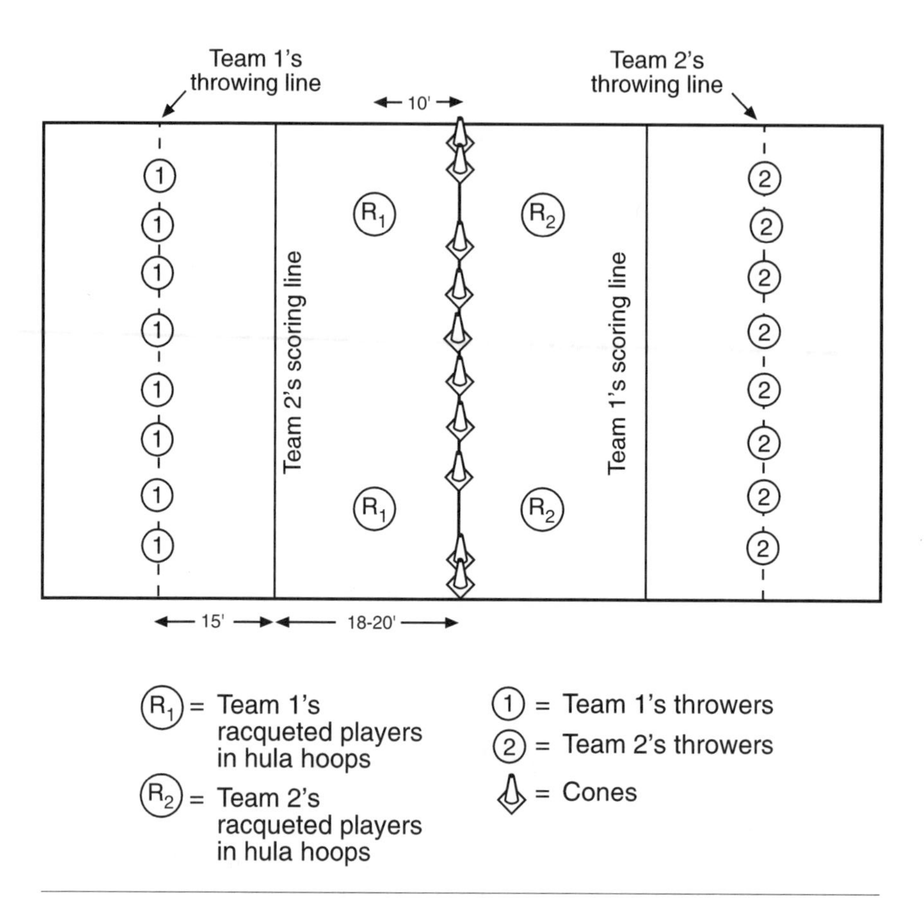

Figure 7.3 Cone Slide Bombardment court design and player setup.

Game

Cones are placed on the centerline of the court. A player with a tennis racket occupies each of the hula hoops on his team's side of the court. These individuals must have both feet within their circles and may not touch the balls, but may use their rackets to deflect, trap, and hit balls. The other eight players must remain on or behind a designated line while aiming for the cones. No exact distance from the centerline to the scoring line or the throwing/kicking line is required. Usually most gyms have a multitude of lines, and selection should be based upon the skill level of the participants, provided both halves of the court have the identical critical markings. Play proceeds in innings of three to four minutes. A cone that is sent over the opponent's scoring line is returned to play at the centerline by a referee after the score is recorded. If a player with a racket steps out of her circle or uses anything but her racket to play the ball, a penalty point is awarded to the opposing team. Thus, circle participants may not touch the balls with their hands or feet, nor are they allowed to contact a cone with their racket.

For variation, play some innings requiring all players, except those with the rackets, to use their preferred hands, non-preferred hands, or feet only to propel the balls. After each inning substitute two other players for those in the hoops. Note, cones that tip over are not reset into an upright position until the end of the inning or until a point is recorded for that cone, whichever comes first.

Safety Considerations

Remind players positioned in the hoops that they are not permitted to throw their rackets at balls or step out of their circles with either foot. If these rules are followed, it is virtually impossible for a player to be inadvertently hit by a racket.

ENDLINE BALL

Participants earn points by sending a ball across the opposing team's endline while preventing their opponents from doing the same on their half of the court. Points are also earned if a ball propelled by an opponent is caught in the air.

Objectives

Reinforces speed, throwing, catching, and kicking skills, as well as eye-hand coordination.

Equipment

Per court, ten cones are used to mark the playing area. Four index cards and four pencils are used by referees to record scores. The variation played dictates the equipment needs. The tennis version requires three tennis balls and eight tennis rackets per court. Three balls of the appropriate type are needed in the soccer, volleyball, or football options. The lacrosse modification requires eight crosses and three tennis balls or eight one-gallon milk jugs with the bottoms removed and three tennis balls. The softball version demands eight gloves and three indoor softballs.

Playing Area

A large grassy field or unobstructed concrete area such as an empty parking lot. The length of the playing area is dictated by the equipment used and the skill level and strength of the participants. Figure 7.4 shows the standard shape of the court and player setup, but the size of the

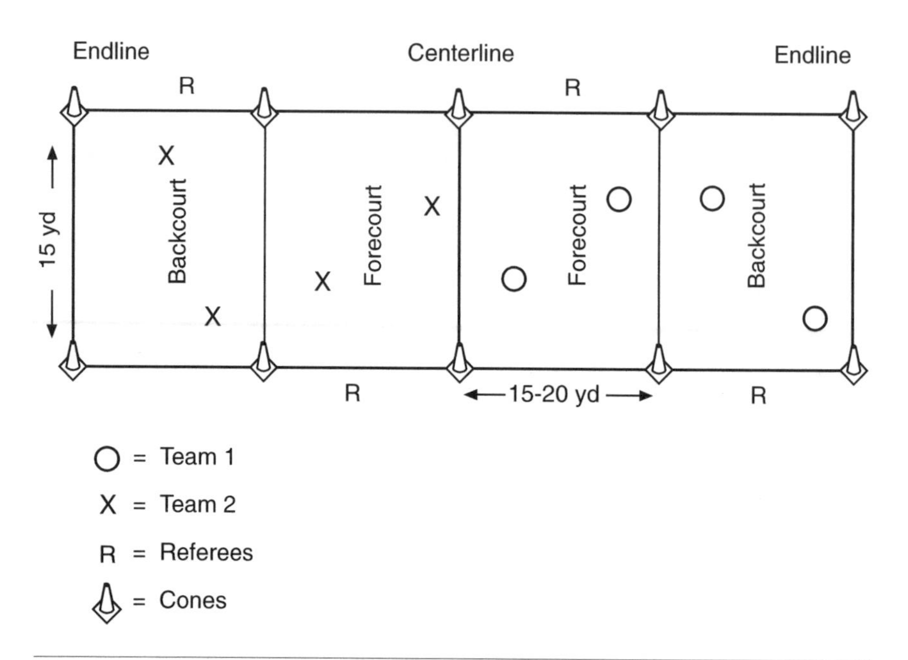

Figure 7.4 Standard Endline Ball court design and player setup. Sizing will vary depending on the motor actions, skill, and strength of participants. Dimensions are for the tennis variation.

back and forecourts must be determined locally by professionals. The dimensions in figure 7.4 are approximations when playing the tennis variation. Separate multiple courts by at least eight yards (7.3 meters).

Participants

Each court will accommodate three teams of four players each; one team will serve as referees.

Game

To begin the game, one ball is placed on the centerline, and one ball is positioned on each endline. The four players from each team are located on the line that separates their team's forecourt from the backcourt. The two players that have been assigned to the forecourt face the centerline, while those that will be playing in the backcourt are facing their endline. On the sound of the whistle, one or both players from each of the four portions of the court runs to the ball.

Balls may be passed among teammates in the backcourt but not the forecourt. Additionally, the ball may be passed from one team's backcourt to its forecourt but not in the reverse direction. Once a ball is brought under control, the player has eight seconds and may take only two steps before the ball is sent into the forecourt of the opponent's half of the playing area, or from one backcourt player to another. Referees should count aloud starting with the number six after five seconds have elapsed. A player may only have one ball in his possession at one time. Thus, if a player has secured a ball, he may not simply drop it on the playing area if another ball is headed in his direction. Violations of any of these provisions results in a penalty point assessed against the team committing the transgression.

If a player catches the ball on a fly that was projected by an opposing team's player, the catcher's team earns two points. When the lacrosse version is played, to earn a point the catch must be made using the crosse or the milk jug, and throughout the game, players are not permitted to touch the ball with their hands. A similar rule pertains to the softball variation in that catches must be made with the glove. When playing the soccer variation, if the ball is not caught on a fly, it must be brought under control using the feet before the ball is allowed to be picked up or else a point is awarded to the opposing team.

For each ball that successfully rolls or crosses over the opponent's endline, three points are earned. For any ball projected across the centerline that rolls out-of-bounds over either sideline in the opponent's forecourt, one point is awarded to the receiving team provided that the ball was not touched by a member of that team. If a ball sent by the opposing team rolls beyond the forecourt sidelines after it is touched by a receiving team's forecourt player, no points are awarded. No points are awarded for balls that cross the sidelines in a team's backcourt. The nearest referee returns balls that cross a sideline by rolling the ball into the portion of the playing area where it went out-of-bounds. Balls that are sent over the endlines are retrieved by a backcourt player.

Play continues in five-minute intervals, after which the teams rotate. One court team becomes the referees, the opposing team moves to the other half of the playing area, and the referees assume the vacated half of the court. The next time the same teams compete, have the individuals who were in the backcourt move to the forecourt, and vice versa. Additionally, swap halves of the field each team was defending. Once each team has played the other twice, total points for each team are compared to determine an overall winner, as are the two innings against each of the other two teams, so a victor can be acknowledged from these sub-competitions.

Helpful Hints

The rules are not really too complex, but because there is no carryover from a similar sport model, it would be easier if key violations and point scoring were written on index cards that officials could refer to during the game. Strategy dictates that if a backcourt player is attempting to retrieve a ball, the opposing team should try to project another ball into the area that individual is supposed to cover or a second ball to that same individual, thus increasing the chance of scoring. If a backcourt player does not hit the ball directly into her opponent's court, then it is important for her to send the ball quickly into the forecourt.

Adaptations for Younger Participants

The easiest action is simply to have players throw a tennis ball, but this will require that the playing area be reduced in size.

FRISBEE SKEET BOWLING

Offensive players attempt to knock down the opposing team's pins by throwing a Frisbee over their team's pins while trying to keep defensive competitors from hitting their projectiles as they travel through the air. Points are scored by the offense for each pin that is toppled; the defense earns points for downing a Frisbee when it enters into a no-fly zone.

Objectives

Enhances eye-hand coordination and a variety of throwing skills. Develops accuracy in spatial-temporal anticipation and prediction and abdominal muscular strength/endurance.

Equipment

Twenty Indian clubs or containers for badminton birds or tennis balls; 12 Frisbees, six of one color and six of another color; 12 foam soccer-sized balls; six scooters; six pinnies, three of one color and three of another color, preferably to match the colors of the Frisbees; and eight cones.

Playing Area

A basketball court, which is divided approximately into thirds. The 10 pins for each team are set up in the middle third of the court, such that there is approximately 30 feet (9.1 meters) separating each team's row of targets. Two cones are placed on the sidelines approximately 15 to 20 feet (4.6 to 6.1 meters) away from the row of pins on each half of the court, depending upon the skill level of the participants. These are the lines behind which the Frisbee throwers must stay. Defenders from one team may locate themselves on portions of both sidelines as long as they remain between the opposing team's Frisbee throwing line and the centerline. Players on scooters generally are permitted to roll anywhere within the court but are positioned within eight feet (2.4 meters) of the lines on which the pins are placed. See figure 7.5 for a diagram of the court and player positioning.

Participants

Fifteen per team and two referees.

Game

Assign one color Frisbee to each team. Each 15-player team is divided into two groups of six. One group plays offense and the other plays

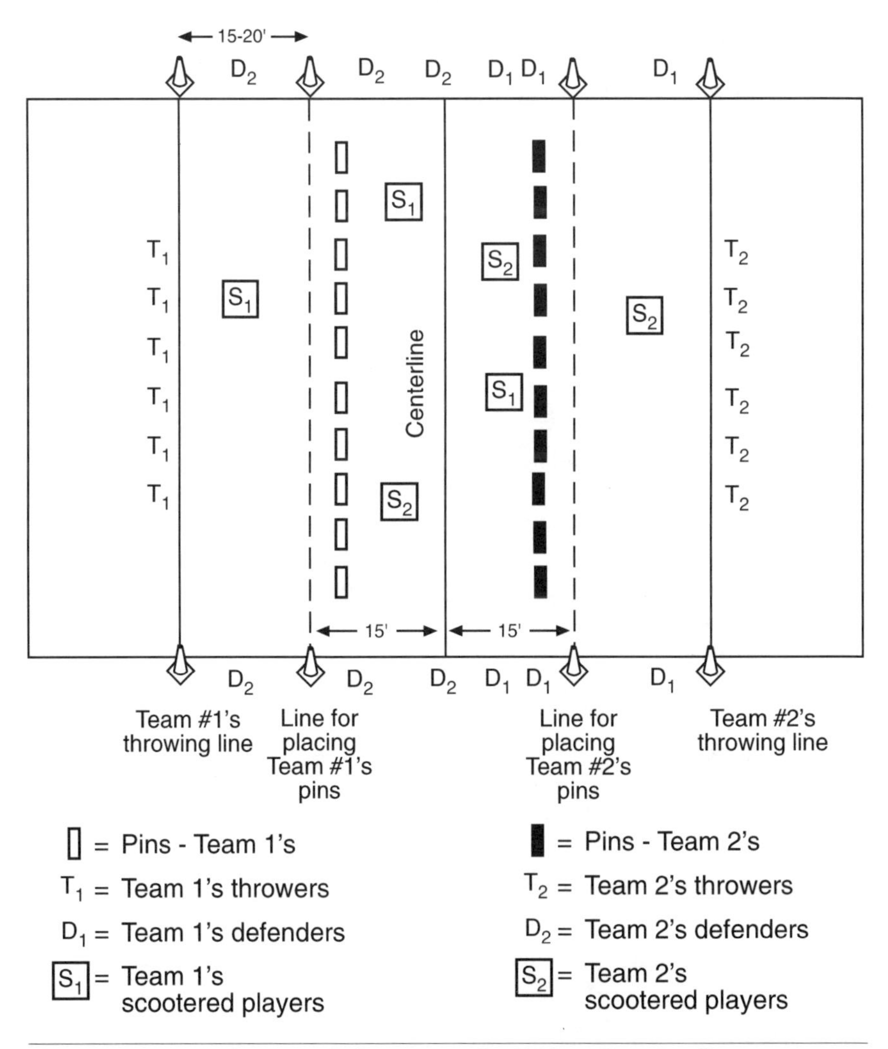

Figure 7.5 Court design and player setup for Frisbee Skeet Bowling.

defense. A group of three players wearing pinnies the same color as their team's Frisbees are on scooters. The players on scooters retrieve and send only their team's disks to their offense. Should a ball land on the court such that a defender would be unable to reach it while standing beyond the sideline, it may be retrieved by a player on a scooter (figure 7.6).

Play continues in rounds of three to four minutes each or until one team has knocked down all of the opponent's pins, whichever occurs first. Players armed with balls track and throw at the opponents' Frisbees. Two points are awarded to the offense for each pin that is toppled by a Frisbee. Two points are awarded to the defense each time the Frisbee is deflected by a ball. Note, it does not matter if a member from one team hits a Frisbee from his own team; the points are awarded based on the color of the Frisbee that was intercepted. For example, if a red Frisbee is shot down, the blue team earns two points, no matter who threw the ball. In essence, if the ball that hit their team's Frisbee was thrown by a member of the same team, they will be penalized for friendly fire. Likewise, if a player on a scooter knocks down one of her team's pins, it is

Figure 7.6 Frisbee Skeet Bowling action where a sideline player is trying to knock a Frisbee down by throwing a ball at the disk before the Frisbee can topple any of the opponent's pins. A player on a scooter gets ready to retrieve the Frisbee and return it to her team.

not reset, and two points are earned by the opposing team. However, should a ball topple one of the pins, it is reset, upon instructions from one of the referees, by a scooter-mounted member from the team whose pin was knocked down.

Occasionally, a player on a scooter will topple one of his opponent's pins. When this occurs it is reset by that person, and two points are awarded to the opposing team. At the end of the inning, the three players on scooters become Frisbee throwers; three of the Frisbee throwers switch to ball throwing; and three of the ball throwers move to the scooters. Thus, after five periods, each person would have had an opportunity to play offense and defense twice, and retrieve on scooters once.

Helpful Hints

Intercepting an object when its trajectory is perpendicular to the direction from which the throw is delivered is not an easy task, even with the slow flight of a Frisbee. Players will need instruction and practice on this technique. The majority of errors will result from timing problems where the ball is released too late for the spot where the player has spatially predicted the target will be located.

HAND-MINTON AND MILK JUG-MINTON

Hand-Minton requires players to execute handball-striking patterns to send a tennis ball over a badminton net while attempting to prevent their opponents from being able to contact and successfully return the ball after no more than one bounce. When milk jugs are employed, a different game emerges, incorporating novel equipment. Because of the similarities in rules, the explanation for Milk Jug-Minton is included here.

Objectives

Develops eye-hand coordination while emphasizing speed and agility. Reinforces bilateral striking patterns (Hand-Minton only).

Equipment

Hand-Minton—one tennis ball per court. Milk Jug-Minton—one tennis ball per court and a one-gallon plastic container with the bottom removed for each player. Both games require badminton poles, a badminton net, and four cones or polyspots.

Playing Area

One badminton court for every two to four participants. On each side of the net, a cone or polyspot is placed 10 feet (3.0 meters) in back of the short service line and at least two feet (0.6 meter) from the doubles side-line outside of the court boundaries.

Participants

Singles or doubles play is possible with either game.

Game

Similar movement patterns, player rotation, and rules are transferred from badminton and will not be reviewed here. In Hand-Minton, the server must let the ball rebound from the floor before using an underhand motion to deliver the serve (figure 7.7). From the contact, the ball must cross over the net and bounce in the service area but no further back than the cone or polyspot. The opponent must let the ball bounce once prior to returning the serve. Thereafter, players may contact the ball after a single bounce or on the fly, such that if the opponent chose to let the ball bounce, it would land within the boundaries of his half of the court. Note, this means that the ball may be played when an individual is standing outside of the court.

In Milk Jug-Minton, the server must toss the ball underhanded using the milk jug so that it lands within the same area specified in Hand-Minton. The receiver must secure the ball from the single bounce before it is returned (figure 7.8). Thereafter, the ball may be caught in the air or after it bounces once within the boundaries of the court. After securing the ball, a player may take only one step before the ball must be sent over the net, but in no case may the ball be returned while a player is located between the net and the short service line. If the ball is caught while a player is in that area, in singles and doubles play, she must return to the "T" (the point where the centerline and short service line intersect) re-

Figure 7.7 Hand-Minton action during a rally.

Figure 7.8 Milk Jug-Minton action during a rally.

gardless of the number of steps needed prior to returning the ball. In doubles play, a second option exists where the individual may toss the ball to her teammate who is located within the court but in back of the short service line. If the ball has not touched the floor on that half of the court since it was last sent over the net, then the teammate is permitted to catch the ball from the partner's toss after one bounce. This is the only condition under which members from the same team may each touch the ball prior to it being returned to the opponents. Occasionally, players will purposely slow down the game and spend too much time between catching and returning the ball. If this occurs, invoke a five-second rule, which is counted aloud by one of the opponents, requiring participants to make their tosses within that time frame once they have secured the ball in their jug. Carries, slings, and double hits are not permitted.

Helpful Hints

Prior to playing Hand-Minton, instructors will need to be certain that participants have developed skills allowing them to return balls with either hand. While it is sometimes possible to succeed by punching the ball, far greater control is maintained by striking the ball with an open hand. Especially during singles play, stress the importance of forcing your opponent to return the ball from the back of the court after the return of serve is completed. When this occurs, most returns, if they are sent over the net, tend to be short and are often prey to a smash.

Milk Jug-Minton should not be attempted before players can catch and demonstrate reasonably accurate throws within a confined area. Because the distance over which the ball can be projected is limited, overhand throwing motions are not used often, as compared to sidearm and underhand tosses. For singles play with highly skilled competitors, consider providing them with two milk jugs, one in each hand. If this is done, a rule may be added permitting the player to transfer the ball into the other jug before returning it to his opponent.

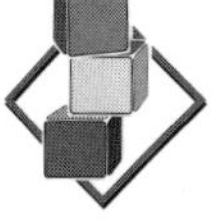

Adaptations for Younger Participants

For Hand-Minton use a small-sized utility ball and lower the net height to approximately four feet (1.2 meters). If these adjustments do not increase the length of rallies, then allow each player to hit the ball once prior to the ball going over the net from the second contact. If the two-hit rule is adopted, then incorporate the following requirements: The same player may not hit the ball twice, and no smashing actions are allowed if the hitter is standing between the net and the short service line.

Providing Multimedia Adaptations

A world of possibilities exists for developing innovative games rooted in ideas found in television, video games, pinball, paper and pencil, and board games.

Television

Contestant-type game shows provide a natural setting that may be modified to some degree to produce activities popular with adolescents. The major change for most programs is incorporating physical activity. Probably the easiest and most direct way to do this is through relay races. The team that completes the relay first gets to answer a question, choose a letter, earn a piece to the puzzle—whatever is appropriate to the game. Even though the relay provides the basic element for movement, participants will perceive the games as different as long as the ultimate goal varies.

Other television programming can give rise to novel activities. For example, action stories can provide the basis for activity, with players imitating the movements of fictitious characters.

Murder mysteries are solved by correct interpretation of a series of clues through deductive reasoning; this concept provides the foundation for Treasure Hunt (Lichtman, 1993). This game requires that participants perform physical activity after they decipher a coded message. The information in one clue leads a team to another clue, followed by another and so on, leading eventually to a reward or treasure.

Video and Pinball Games

The recent rage in home entertainment has been video games, a technological spin-off from pinball machines. The themes common to these computerized wonders are no different from most games played on the court or in the gym: score more points than your opponent, eclipse your personal record, complete a task within a given time frame, or render your opponent helpless before she or he forces you into the same state. It is simply the context in which these goals are achieved that makes them appear unique. That is the essence of what you must capitalize on: By transferring context from the screen to the playground, you may create a seemingly novel activity.

It is usually impossible to translate every aspect of your model video or pinball game into the new activity. Focus instead on carrying over the major theme—lack of predictability and the possibility of losing control of the object that is the primary vehicle for scoring points. To achieve this, modify selected areas to adapt the game to your setting.

Recreational Board Games

You also may develop innovative games by modifying recreational board games to fit within a gymnasium setting. For example, take the idea behind the game of Battleship, which is to sink the enemy's craft before its forces can destroy your own. You may use tin cans as the targets and balls for torpedoes or missile shells. To enhance the element of suspense, restrict the players' vision by draping sheets over nets at badminton height.

The critical element for transferring ideas from board, video, or pinball games or from television game shows into an activity that includes movement is an open mind that asks, "How can the basic premise of this show or game be adapted to a physical setting?" By using and thinking about the examples of activities in this section, you should gain greater insight into how to succeed in creating your own games.

The Games

The games within this chapter are arranged according to the amount of physical activity required during play, with the last activity, Roller Trash Can Basketball, being the most demanding.

TIC-TAC-TOE MULTIPLE WAYS

A host of possibilities exists for modifying the paper and pencil version of Tic-Tac-Toe into one that requires sport skills. In each instance, the goal is the same: Secure a line of three squares before your opponent can do so. Variations are developed based upon the type of motor actions demanded, which in some instances are dependent upon the specific nature of the playing area.

Objectives

Develops accuracy of eye-hand coordination through various propulsive actions.

Equipment

Indoor courts require tape or washable poster paint and a brush 1.5 inches (3.8 centimeters) wide. For a more permanent court, the Tic-Tac-Toe design could be painted or taped on some heavy cloth or brown wrapping paper. For outdoor play, use chalk. For each court, you will need eight poker chips in each of two different colors, to mark the boxes a player earns and four polyspots to designate a line behind which players must remain when aiming at the grid. Other equipment needs are dependent upon the version that is played. Both pitch and hit variations require one tennis ball or racquetball per court. For the badminton modification, two badminton rackets and two shuttlecocks per court are required. If the badminton version is played in a hallway, a piece of string long enough to tape to the walls will simulate a badminton net.

Playing Area

The Pitch and Hit version and the Badminton version may be played anywhere there is an unobstructed area measuring approximately 6 by 28 feet (1.8 by 8.5 meters). The Pitch, Hit, and Rebound variation requires the same size court, but an unobstructed wall must be located within two to three feet (0.6 to 0.9 meter) on at least one side of the court. The size of the Tic-Tac-Toe grid for each of the above variations is three by three feet (0.9 by 0.9 meter) with each square measuring one by one foot (0.3 by 0.3 meter). Most school or recreational building hallways are ideal, as in most cases corridors are narrow enough to permit rebounds from either wall and a string may be taped to the walls to simulate the height of a badminton net. Figure 8.1 depicts the basic court design with one wall present.

Participants

Two or four players per court.

Game

With four participants per playing area, assign one person from each team to each end of the court. Assign the players behind one of the endlines to be the pitchers or servers, while those on the opposite side will aim for the target. Those serving/pitching alternate sending the shuttle or ball to the opposing player on the opposite side of the court until one team has won. Then without changing ends of the court (except as noted for Pitch, Hit, and Rebound play), the roles will be reversed. Pitchers, servers, and hitters are not permitted to step across their endline prior to release or contact. Violation by the pitcher or server

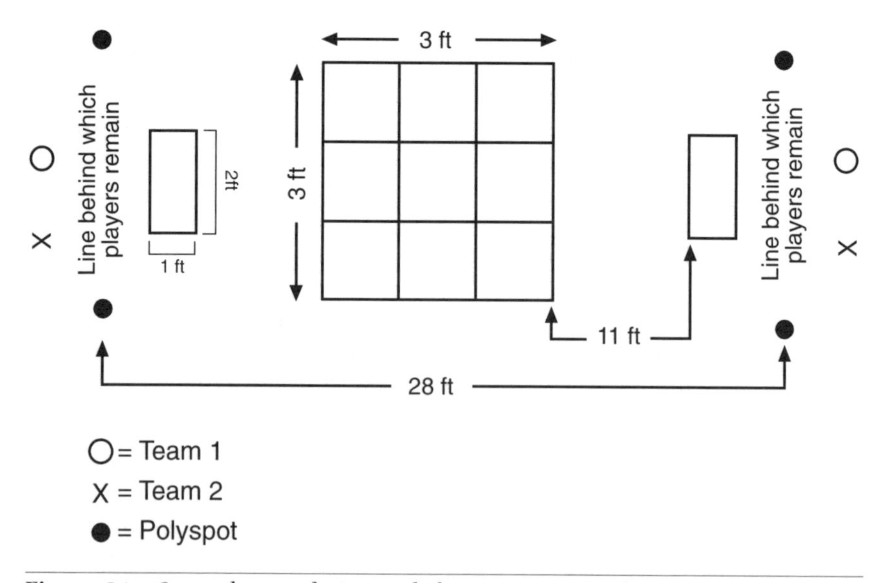

Figure 8.1 General court design and player positioning for Tic-Tac-Toe when played indoors.

results in an error. If the hitter who is aiming at the target commits a violation, no box is earned, regardless of where the object landed, and a second chance is not given.

Pitch and Hit and Pitch, Hit, and Rebound Versions

The ball is pitched using an underhand toss so that the ball reaches a height of about waist level during its trajectory. The first bounce must be in the box immediately in front of the hitter. If the ball fails to land in that area, a second pitch is delivered. If two consecutive pitches miss, the hitting team may place a poker chip in any square of the Tic-Tac-Toe grid or may remove one of the other team's chips. If the ball bounces in the box, the hitter must strike the ball with a hand, attempting to have the ball land on an empty box of the Tic-Tac-Toe grid. If the ball bounces in the box and the hitter swings and misses or does not attempt to swing at all, a violation occurs, and the opposing team prepares to hit. Three out of five games determines the winner. Balls or shuttles landing on one or more of the Tic-Tac-Toe lines are not considered good. After each two games, have players from one team change ends so that each will get to pitch to a different opponent. If the match goes to a fifth game, each team may decide which member will be the hitter and which will pitch.

If the ball lands in one of the squares and

- no chip is present, the hitting team places a chip in that area.
- one of the hitting team's chips is already there, play continues.
- the opponent's chip was placed in that position during that team's last at bat, the opponent's chip is removed. (Note, it is not replaced with a chip from the opposing team.)
- the opponent's chip is already there but was not positioned during that team's last at bat, play continues.

In the Pitch and Hit variation, the hitter must send the ball directly onto the Tic-Tac-Toe court, while in the Pitch, Hit, and Rebound modification, the hitter must propel the ball to a wall and have it ricochet onto the court. For both games, where the ball lands on its first bounce on the playing surface after contact determines the outcome. Hitting the ball across one's body is far easier than propelling the ball to the wall that is on the same side as the hand a player uses for contacting. In this case, if the court does not have walls on each side, let participants change ends after each game.

Badminton Version

Play is similar to that described for Pitch and Hit play, except that an underhand short serve is delivered and the opponent must legally hit the shuttle. If a string is used to simulate net height, then the serve as well as the return must clear the net to be considered in play. The hitter may opt to contact the shuttle even though it would not have landed in the box in front of the endline, had he let the bird fall to the floor. If the player opts to let the shuttle drop to the floor and it does not land in the box, an errant serve results. After three consecutive errant serves, the hitting team may place a poker chip in any square of the board or may remove one of the other team's chips. Wherever the shuttle comes to rest is the position that is used to ascertain whether the serve was good or if the return resulted in the team successfully hitting the shuttle into a given square. If the hitter lets the shuttle hit the playing surface in the box in front of the endline, a violation results and the opposing team goes on the offense.

Safety Considerations

With four on a court, remind players who are waiting their turn to provide adequate space for unimpeded play.

Helpful Hints

Other variations of this same game are possible; however, those that appear in table 8.1 are played on grass, using a larger court, with expanded dimensions for the Tic-Tac-Toe board.

For variations in table 8.1, since no pitching/serving occurs, have opposing players from each endline alternately aim at the target while the other players return the projected object to their teammates and mark the square in which the object lands.

Table 8.1

Additional Tic-Tac-Toe Variations

Motor skill	Equipment	Modification of playing area
Soccer kick	Two soccer balls	Grassy area; chalked squares are 3 by 3 ft (0.9 by 0.9 m); endlines are 30-35 ft (9.1-10.7 m) from the center square; use plastic cups instead of chips
Underhand roll	Two playground balls or two soccer balls	Same as above
Frisbee throw	Two Frisbees	Grassy area; squares are 4 by 4 ft (1.2 by 1.2 m); endlines are 40-45 ft (12.2-13.7 m) from the center square; use plastic cups instead of chips

Motor skill	Equipment	Modification of playing area
Fungo-hitting	Two plastic bats and two Wiffle balls or two bats and two mushballs	Grassy area; squares are 2 by 2 ft (0.6 by 0.6 m); endlines are 60-75 ft (18.3-22.9 m) from the center square; use plastic cups instead of chips
Putting/chipping	Two putters or two wedges and two golf balls	Grassy area suitable for putting or chipping; for putting, each chalked square is 6 by 6 in. (15 by 15 cm) and the distance from the endlines to the center square is 15-20 ft (4.6-6.1 m); for chipping, each square is 1 by 1 ft (0.3 by 0.3 m) and the endlines are 30-35 ft (9.1-10.7 m) from the center square; use chips
Horseshoes/ washers	Two horseshoes or two washers 1-1/2 in. (3.8 cm)	Grassy area; chalked squares are 1 by 1 ft (0.3 by 0.3 m); distance from the endlines to the center square is 15-20 ft (4.6-6.1 m); use chips

BATTLESHIP

Participants roll balls, which simulate torpedoes, at the opposition's hidden targets (battleships), trying to sink all enemy boats before all of their team's battleships have been destroyed.

Objectives

Enhances kicking, rolling, and throwing skills, while it reinforces agility, speed, and precise communication between players.

Equipment

A volleyball net or badminton net and two poles, with the net set at a height of six to six and a half feet (1.8 to 2 meters). Three or four sheets that are draped over the net so the lowest point for each is approximately 18 inches (0.5 meter) off the floor. Also needed are between 20 and 30 objects with lids that can be knocked over or displaced. These could include badminton tubes, pins, tennis ball containers, one-pound coffee cans, frozen juice cans, and so on. Place a small quantity of dried beans or peas in each and secure the lids with duct tape. Identical sets of containers are needed with different types of receptacles worth varying points. For example, scoring might range from one point for coffee cans to three points for badminton tubes and so on. Eight to ten foam soccer-sized balls, with six or eight of one color and the others of a different color. Two index cards, each with a list of tasks such as 15 push-ups, 15 squat thrusts, 15 blastoffs, 15 mule kicks, and so on, taped behind and centered with the baseline of each team.

Playing Area

A volleyball or badminton court.

Participants

Ten players per team when played on a volleyball court, with three participants serving as retrievers, two as lookouts who communicate where the opposing team's ships are located, and the remaining five court players defending their targets and also attempting to down the opponents' ships. On a badminton court, each team of eight is comprised of two retrievers, two lookouts, and four court players. See figure 8.2 for Battleship court setup and player positioning. There are two referees, one for each side of the court.

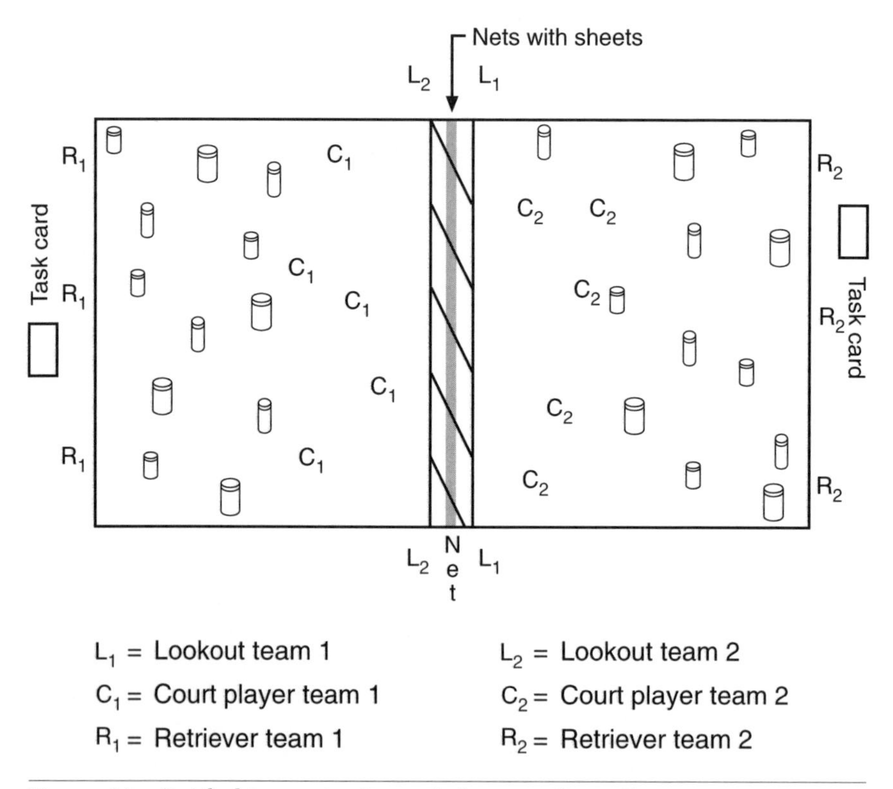

Figure 8.2 Battleship court setup and player configuration.

Game

Court players may not go beyond their side- or endlines. Retrievers and lookouts are not permitted on the court but must stay on their side of the net. Generally one lookout is positioned near each pole and retrievers are located behind the endline. Each team places its containers on its half of the court, with the restriction that no two containers may be within four to five feet (1.2 to 1.5 meters) of each other. To begin the game, the balls are placed along the centerline directly under the sheets and the court players are located at the baseline. Designate the six to eight balls of one color as those that can be sent either under or over the net, while balls of the other color may be sent only over the net. At the whistle, court players rush forward and, without touching the balls with their hands, must get each one to their baseline before they can be used to down the opponent's targets. Note, retrievers may assist with this. Once a ball has reached the baseline, court players may use their hands. Lookouts tell court players where to aim.

Additional Rules

A player committing an offense must go behind her team's baseline and complete a task of her choosing from the list on the index card for each of the following violations:

- A player sends a ball under the net when the ball is required to be thrown over the sheets.
- A lookout plays the ball.
- A retriever throws the ball to the opponent's court.
- A court player crosses the sidelines or goes beyond the endline, unless he was completing a task from the list.
- A court player or retriever attempts to look under or over the net.
- A ball is caught on the fly by an opposing court player or retriever (the thrower is at fault).
- A ball hits any part of an opponent on the fly (the player who was contacted is at fault).

Should a court player knock down a container while attempting to stop an opponent's shot, the ship is considered destroyed. Any toppled vessel should be removed by the court players, who should place it well beyond the endline so that it doesn't happen to hit another container. Each round or inning is four minutes in duration. Points are awarded based on the difference between the number of targets that remain standing between the teams. Court players alternate positions with the lookouts and retrievers after each inning.

Helpful Hints

Encourage players to avoid setting targets on existing lines within the court, especially if the pattern of lines is duplicated on the other half of the playing area. Lookouts should signal their team's court players when and where to throw or kick balls in order to catch the defense off guard. To reduce the chances of having a ball that must be thrown over the net being caught by an opposing court player or retriever, participants should approach the net in a spiking fashion and propel the ball downward with a great deal of force.

POLE FOOSBALL

While holding a piece of PVC pipe, pairs attempt to propel balls across a team's endline into a goal using a typical foosball-type positioning.

Objectives

Develops cooperation, eye-hand coordination, kicking, and unique swinging and contacting motor patterns.

Equipment

Twenty-eight 8- to 10-foot (2.4- to 3.0-meter) sections of one-inch (2.5-centimeter) PVC piping. At each end, one-third-inch (0.85-centimeter) holes are drilled and a piece of quarter-inch (0.64-centimeter) rope about one foot (0.3 meter) long is secured through each hole to form a thong. Ten lighter weight medium-sized balls such as volleyballs, foam soccer balls, or beachballs. Twenty-four pinnies and four cones.

Playing Area

A football field or other field that has been lined in five-yard (4.6-meter) increments using an area of approximately 65 yards by 25 yards (59.4 by 22.9 meters). Figure 8.3 shows the field setup and the player location.

Participants

Eighty-four participants, divided into three teams. One team serves as the referees for the other two teams. Fewer participants may be accommodated by eliminating two lines of players on each half of the field, by having some alleys with only one pair of players, including only one pair in the goal, or by reducing the width of the playing field to about 15 yards (13.7 meters) and playing with only one pair per five-yard (4.6-meter) increment. Regardless of the number involved, there must be an even number of balls used, and the same number of alleys must be located on each half of the field.

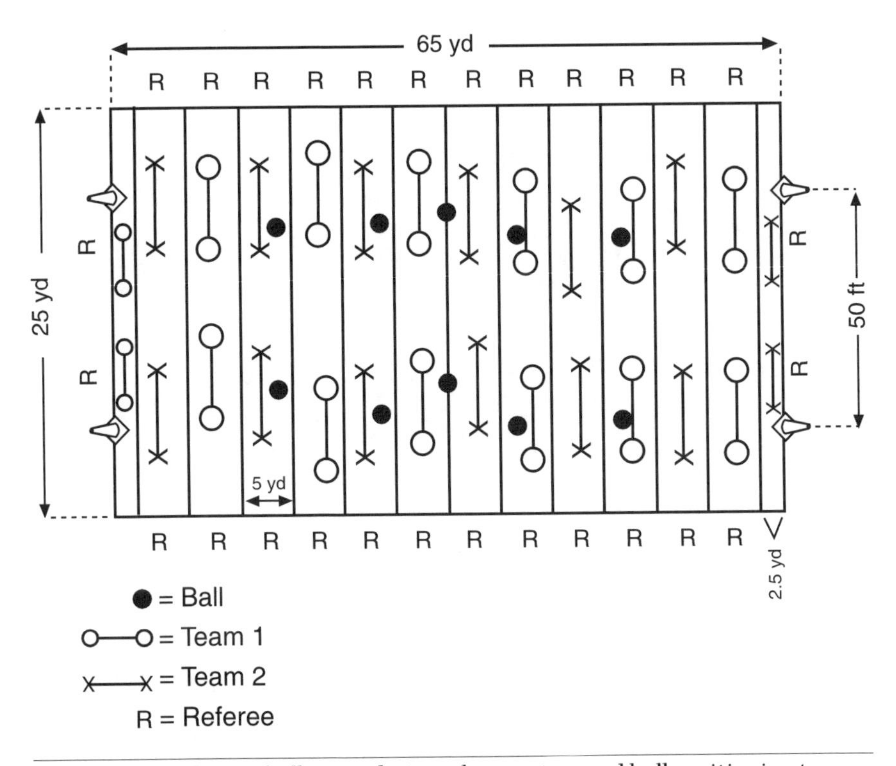

Figure 8.3 Pole Foosball court design, player setup, and ball positioning to start an inning.

Game

After positioning players and referees as shown in figure 8.3, begin a five-minute inning by positioning one ball in front of each pole on the first two offensive lines on each half of the court. Two balls should be placed on the centerline. A player may face in either direction but must have at least one hand through the thong. Holding onto the pole with the free hand is permitted. Court players are permitted to use their poles or any part of their bodies except their hands to contact the balls (figure 8.4). Goalies may use their free hands. Players must remain completely within their five-yard (4.6-meter) alley. A ball must pass between the two cones to be scored a goal.

Should a hand ball occur (where the free hand of a court player contacts the ball), the referee observing the violation will secure the ball and roll it into the opposing team's alley adjacent to the one where the player committed the error but closer to the opposing team's goal. Balls that are sent out-of-bounds over the sidelines are returned in a like manner. A ball that is sent over the endline or into the goal is passed from referee to referee until it crosses the centerline where it is rolled into the

Figure 8.4 Action in Pole Foosball using the pole to send a ball past opponents playing in an adjacent alley.

playing area of the first line of players on that half of the playing area. The goal referees keep track of time and the number of goals scored.

After five minutes of continuous play, the teams rotate so there is a new group of referees. The players whose team remains on the playing field will switch ends of the field, from offense to defense and vice versa. The team that had served as officials now become court players. A game consists of six innings. The rotation system is similar to a round-robin. Each team will play against each of the other two teams twice, with players dividing their time between offensive and defensive play. Each team will also serve as referees twice within the game's six innings. Table 8.2 explains the proper rotational patterns.

Additional Rules

If a player repeatedly and intentionally crosses into another zone, crosses into the goal area, or purposely drops the pole while playing the ball,

Table 8.2

Rotational Sequence for Pole Foosball and Roller Trash Can Basketball

Inning	Offense	Defense	Referees
1	A-1, B-1	A-2, B-2	C
2	B-1, C-1	B-2, C-2	A
3	C-1, A-1	C-2, A-2	B
4	B-2, A-2	B-1, A-1	C
5	C-2, B-2	C-1, B-1	A
6	A-2, C-2	A-1, C-1	B

A, B, and C represent teams. A-1 and A-2 represent the two halves of team A. A similar pattern follows for teams B and C.

both players on that pole lose the privilege of playing with their feet for the remainder of that inning. If the action resulted in a goal, the score is disallowed.

If a goalie interferes with an opposing team's players from the alley immediately in front of the goal or purposely drops the pole when playing a ball, a goal is awarded to the opposing team, regardless of whether or not the shot would have resulted in a goal.

Safety Considerations

Check thongs before the poles are used. Remind players that they may change the hand that is put through the rope, but they may not play the balls unless the thong is around one hand. Do not substitute bamboo poles for the PVC piping, as bamboo is easily split and is extremely dangerous.

Helpful Hints

Allow students a short practice period so that they can figure out how best to use the poles and develop a system by which they can communicate with their partner to know when to change thong hands or face a different direction. Instruct players that they will not have success if they attempt to scoop the pole under the ball if it is stationary or rolling on the ground. With the ball in these positions, players should use their pole to strike the center of the ball that is facing toward them. Poles are often used to stop a rolling ball or one which is in the air, so a player can then use her feet, but in doing that, an element of surprise is eliminated.

Variation

Players may use only their poles or only their feet to contact balls, and goalies are unable to use their free hand but may still use their feet and poles.

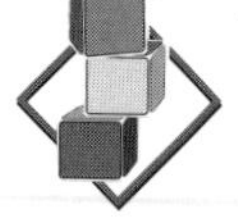

Adaptations for Younger Participants

Reduce the size of the poles to five feet (1.5 meters) for grades three to five and either add a third pair for each zone or narrow the playing field to 15 yards (13.7 meters). If only one pair per zone is used, the field width should be about 10 yards (9.1 meters).

ACTION CLUE

Groups of students attempt to complete a designated task in a set amount of time so that they can receive a clue that will help them to identify a famous athlete, sport, team, and so on. The team providing the most correct answers within the class period is declared the winner.

Objectives

These are dependent upon the types of activities that are selected. Suggested options include:

- Motor fitness and physical fitness actions: Squat thrusts, sit-ups, push-ups, jumping over a line and back, dashes, and agility movements.
- Motor skills: Basketball dribbling, shooting, and passing to a wall; volleyball bumping and overhead passing; throwing and fielding; and soccer dribbling and passing to a wall.

Equipment

Eight to 12 polyspots of a specific color to designate the positions of the different stations. On each marking spot is an index card describing the actions, along with a picture to help participants understand what is required at that station. A listing of station numbers that have been randomly selected with replacement (meaning that a given station number may be selected any number of times) is printed on an index card kept by the instructor. The rest of the equipment will depend upon which actions are included and, for some stations, the number of individuals in each group. The following provides an example of 12 stations with 15 different groups of four participants each. The marking spots alluded to in table 8.3 should be of a different color than those mentioned above.

Table 8.3

A Twelve-Station Action Clue Setup

Station #	Activity description	Equipment needed	Goal in 2 min
1	Jumping over a line and back all holding hands	None	150
2	Basketball dribbling	Five cones, one polyspot, one basketball	10 trips for team total
3	Dash around cone	One cone, one polyspot	14 trips for team total
4	Soccer passing to a wall	One soccer ball, one polyspot	25 made for team total
5	Throwing and fielding to a wall	One tennis ball, one polyspot	35 made for team total
6	Jumping rope	Four speed ropes	140 each
7	Squat thrusts	None	15 each
8	Skipping around cone	One cone, one polyspot	12 trips for team total
9	Lay-ups	One basketball, one polyspot	15 made for team total
10	Volleyball bump or pass to a wall	One volleyball	20 made for team total
11	Soccer dribbling	One soccer ball, four cones, one polyspot	8 trips for team total
12	Basketball wall pass	One basketball, one polyspot	25 made for team total

Figure 8.5 shows how these stations can easily be positioned on one basketball court.

At each station, have the same number of copies of a specific clue for that round as the total number of groups involved in the activity. To distinguish between rounds, place all of one round's clues on paper of the same color. Thus, if three rounds will be played with 15 groups, then round one might be designated by clues on blue paper, round two on white, and round three on yellow. Then each station would have 15 copies of the same clue printed on blue sheets, 15 copies of a different clue that will be used in round two, and so on. Clues are short and generally fit on less than one typed line, so only a small strip of paper is needed for each clue.

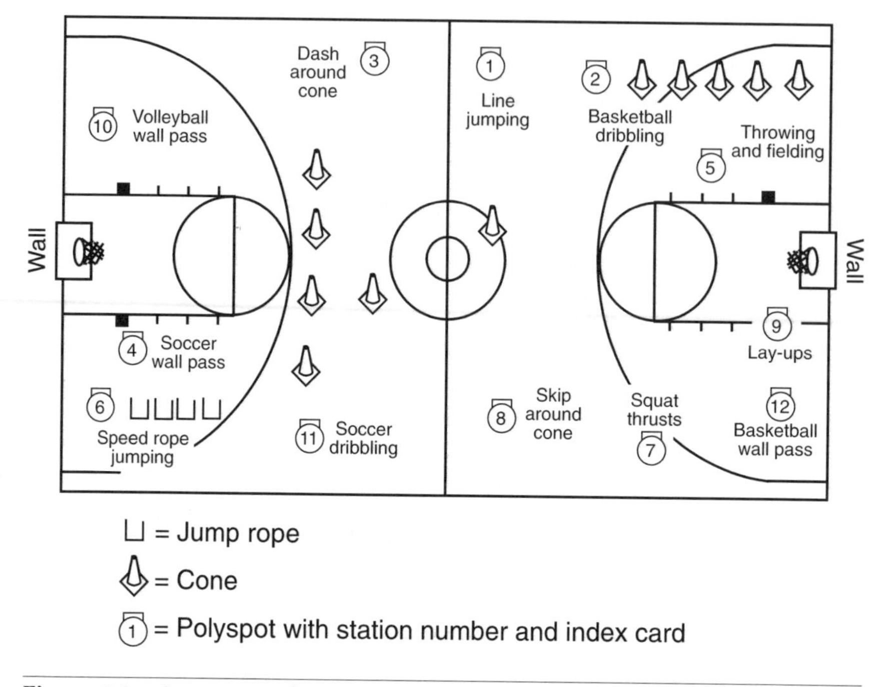

Figure 8.5 Court setup for a 12-station Action Clue.

Participants

Three to five participants at each station, but there will be two to three more groups than stations, as these individuals will serve as the referees.

Game

Divide the class based upon the number of stations you are planning and the information presented above under Participants. Have each person in a group assign himself a letter, starting with A. Have participants move to a spot on one of the boundary lines of the basketball court. It is unimportant whether or not members of a given group stay in the same vicinity together. However, participants should leave at least four to five feet (1.2 to 1.5 meters) between themselves and another individual. The leader announces which color clues will be used in the round. When the signal is given, all participants begin walking or jogging around the outside of the basketball court as instructed. After a delay of up to 20 seconds, the instructor calls out a letter. The individuals who were assigned that letter run as quickly as possible to a colored polyspot which designates a station. Because there will be two to three fewer spots than there are people with the same letter, a situation similar to musical chairs results. Those groups that did not get to a polyspot serve as the referees with each member of these groups going to a different station, or if there are extras, they should be sent to station #6 or #7, where every member would be performing those tasks individually but at the same time.

The rest of the members from the groups that secured a polyspot first join their teammates at that specific station. The groups are given about 30 seconds to read the index card and get organized. At the sound of the whistle, participants begin to do their assigned activity. The instructor keeps time, and after two minutes another whistle blows, ceasing the action. Each group that has successfully completed the station's minimum activity requirements takes the appropriate colored clue for that round.

Members of any team that would like to guess the answer must raise their hands and then do so aloud so the entire class can hear what is said. In the event more than one team wants to answer, the instructor refers to the first randomly selected station number on her index card. Beginning with that station, the referee goes around the gym clockwise, giving any group that wants it a turn to guess. The first group with the correct answer is the winner of that round. In most cases, it takes at least three to four different clues to be able to make a reasonable guess. To begin another sequence, again have all group members, including those who just served as referees, move to a spot on one of the boundary lines of the basketball court and follow the same procedure specified earlier. Note, be sure to inform participants that they do not want to repeat the same station for this given round, unless their team was not successful during a prior attempt, because there is only one specific clue at each station per round. Teams should take the clues they have earned with them, so they can build enough hints to guess effectively.

The following are examples of clues that could be used to depict a famous athlete. The number reflects the station number at which the clue would be located.

John Elway

1. Doesn't kick.
2. Plays on a field.
3. Offense.
4. Plays where it is very cold.
5. Team mascot is a horse.
6. Male.
7. Was still playing in January 1998.
8. Doesn't like to run.
9. A field general.
10. Rarely scores.
11. Plays in back of a line.
12. Will retire in the next two years.

Michelle Kwan

1. Very slender.
2. Participates where it is always cold.
3. Her equipment must be very sharp.
4. Uses two single runners.
5. Female.
6. Saw a lot of White Ring.
7. Never lived in Houston.
8. Needs music.
9. Should compete in 2002.
10. All that glitters is not gold.
11. Does actions that sound like klutz.
12. Sits and often spins.

Other possibilities exist, including specific sports. These are usually easier to figure out.

Baseball

1. Played indoors or outdoors.
2. Needs a ball with seams.
3. Players of this game are sometimes given four.
4. Fouls are called.
5. Helmets needed.
6. Played day or night.
7. National versus American.
8. Long season.
9. Every game a stretch.
10. Peanuts and Cracker Jacks.
11. Invented by an American.
12. Only four let in per year.

Clues may be abstract, as seen in #4 for Michelle Kwan, or straightforward as in #11 for baseball. The more direct the clues, the faster the groups will be able to provide correct answers. Sometimes it is difficult to devise enough subtle clues that don't automatically provide the answer. This is especially true when you have many stations. If it seems impossible to create an adequate number of appropriate verbal clues, consider a picture or carryover from a film. For the baseball example, you might write, "Girls had one of their own" or "The dreaming fields." If this still proves difficult, then another option is to leave some clues blank.

Helpful Hints

Remind participants that they should not reveal the clue to another group, including the referees. A group that is provided with a clue without having to earn it by successfully completing a station gains a tremendous advantage.

Adaptations for Younger Participants

Reduce the organizational complexity by having all groups of five to six performing the identical action at the same time in relay fashion. This will eliminate the need to have participant referees, allowing the entire class to be active at once. With the teacher acting as the referee, the job will be made easier if players round a cone and return to the start/finish line to tag off. Rather than only the winning team being given a clue, consider expanding this so the first half of the groups to finish the relay will receive a clue. Another option is to set a maximum time limit for each team to complete its relay. Any team that is successful is given a new clue. If either of these procedures are followed, create a clue set for each group, making sure the clues are ordered identically for each group. Upon success in a relay, the next clue in sequence is provided to that group.

For second and third graders, decrease the abstractness by providing a puzzle piece of a well-known person, place, or thing, instead of receiving a clue. Puzzle pieces can be made by placing a picture on card stock, then cutting each piece into 9 or 12 squares or, if desired, in jigsaw fashion. Pieces from each picture are placed in a separate paper bag for each relay team, and the bags are located 6 to 8 feet (1.8 to 2.4 meters) in back of each line. Upon success, a designated player from each group selects a piece at random, while the other members gather around. Other groups will be prevented from seeing another team's puzzle pieces if the bag is laid over the pieces that have been earned.

In each of these adapted versions, use an arbitrary way to determine which team will be allowed to guess first when more than one group wishes to attempt a solution. Again, for each round, a different set of clues or puzzle pieces is required.

ROLLER TRASH CAN BASKETBALL

Modification of an activity seen on the television show "American Gladiators." Requires players on scooters to deposit or shoot foam balls into trash cans and basketball hoops as defenders attempt to prevent shots from being taken. The game is played using time periods of four to five minutes. Once a ball has touched the playing surface, it can no longer be used unless a non-shooting offensive player returns it to one of the ball caches.

Objectives

Develops abdominal strength as well as shooting and passing skills.

Equipment

One scooter per player, with 20 to 24 per court; 10 to 12 pinnies, of which 3 or 4 must be of a different color to designate the offensive non-shooters' positions. Two foam soccer-sized balls for each of the offensive shooters. Six 40- to 50-gallon (151.4- to 189.2-liter) plastic trash cans with weighted objects placed inside for stability, and two hula hoops.

Playing Area

An indoor basketball court, with the equipment positioned as seen in figure 8.6.

If two half-court games are played simultaneously, the ball caches should be located at the centerline.

Participants

For full court play, 20 to 24 players can be accommodated. If two half-court games are set up, 12 to 14 players are needed. The number of referees used should be the same as the number of players on one team.

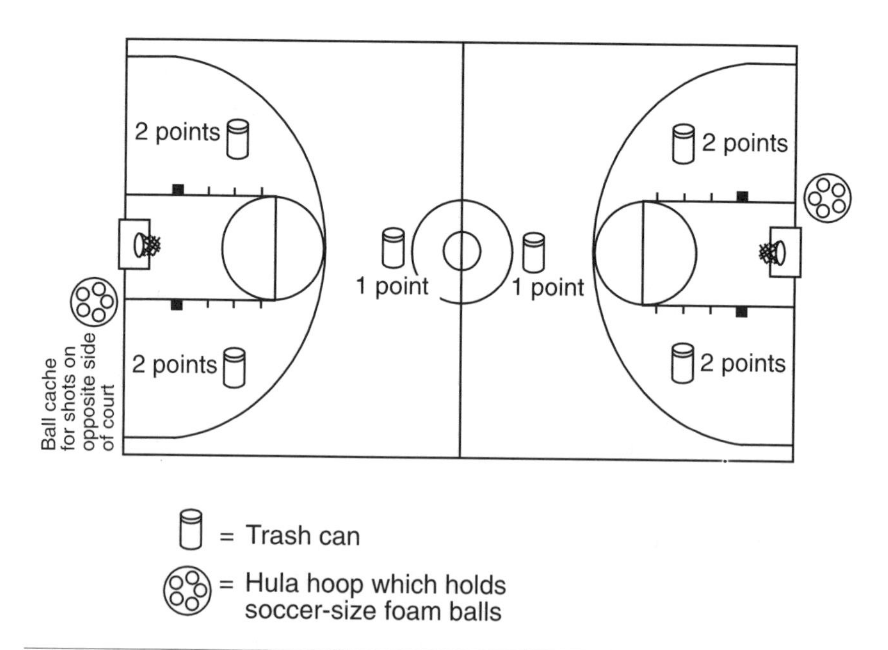

Figure 8.6 Court setup for Roller Trash Can Basketball.

Refereeing assignments can include one referee per trash can, one to monitor each ball cache, one to observe shots taken at each basket, and one or two to monitor general action on each half of the court.

Game

Divide the group into three equal-sized teams, each containing between 10 and 12 players. The offensive team consists of at least seven to eight shooters and three to four non-shooters, with the defense consisting of the same number of players. The shooters are distinguished from the non-shooters by the color of pinnies that are worn. At the opening of each inning, half of the balls are placed in each hoop, and the shooters and non-shooters are divided as evenly as possible and positioned on each endline. The defense is spread out over the entire court. At the whistle, each shooter takes a ball from the nearest hoop and proceeds to move the ball down court by rolling it along the ground.

Once a shooter picks up the ball, he has three options: pass it to a non-shooter on his team, or if he has moved to the opposite half of the court from which the ball had been taken from the cache, he may shoot for a trash can or the basketball hoop (figure 8.7). Thus unless a shooter has crossed the centerline, no points can be earned as only the goals on the far half of the court can be used to score points.

Once the ball hits the ground, it may not be played again until one of the non-shooting offensive players returns it to one of the ball caches. If a non-shooter catches the ball, then that person may either play the ball by rolling with it along the playing surface or throwing it to a member of her team. If a player rolls more than three feet (0.9 meter) while holding

Figure 8.7 Roller Trash Can Basketball action.

the ball, it is considered traveling, and the ball must immediately be placed on the playing surface.

Shooters must alternate the cache from which they take a ball to put into play. If they fail to obey this rule, no points can be scored with that ball. Only shooters are permitted to remove balls from caches and score points. One point is earned for each ball that lands in either of the trash cans closest to the centerline. Two points are awarded for shots made into any of the other four cans, while three points are given for balls shot into the basketball hoops. Should a player attempt any shot and the ball rebounds so that an offensive player catches it in the air, the ball is still considered in play.

Cans may not be dislodged from their original positions. Inadvertent contact that does not provide an advantage to either team is ignored. However, if an offensive player happens to move a can and score when that individual would not have been able to do so if the receptacle had remained in its original position, the bucket is disallowed. If the situation is reversed and the defender hitting the trash can causes the shot to be missed, the referee places the ball in the can, and points are awarded.

Each person must remain on his scooter to be able to play the ball. If a defender collides with an offensive player who is in possession of a ball, the offensive player maintains possession after she gets repositioned on the scooter, even if the ball touched the floor. If this occurred while in the act of shooting and was of sufficient force to dislodge the shooter, the referee immediately places the ball in the can.

It is considered legal for the defense to knock away a ball that is on the playing floor, pick one up and then toss it elsewhere, or do the same with a ball he has caught. However, if in throwing the ball to another area of the court, an offensive player catches the ball on a fly, that ball can immediately be put into play without first being returned to one of the caches by a non-shooter. Defenders are not permitted to touch any ball that is within a cache. The penalty for doing so is removal from the game for two minutes. If the inning ends before the full two minutes elapses, then the remainder of the penalty is enforced during the next inning when that individual's team goes on the offense.

Teams should switch shooter and non-shooter positions so that no individual has to play more than two innings as a non-shooter. Additionally, referees who did not observe play at one of the trash cans should do so when refereeing a second time. Since defenders usually protect a can or general area of the court, responsibilities should be rotated when the defensive role is resumed.

Points are accumulated over each inning and against each team. This allows for an overall class winner, as well as a comparison of how each team performed against each of the other teams.

Helpful Hints

Shooters should be sure that non-shooting offensive players are ready to receive their passes, as a number of balls will be in play at the same time. Shooters should also be sure to require non-shooting offensive players to return a ball that has hit the playing surface to a cache to avoid decreasing the chances for scoring. If non-shooters can set a post with their backs to the trash can, a shooter can often get a clear shot if the ball is passed to the post and the post feeds the ball to the shooter, who is moving toward the basket at a different angle.

Utilizing Unique Locales and Underused Spaces

Physical education teachers and recreational specialists often find themselves needing to accommodate large numbers of participants within a limited amount of space. Many of the innovative activities outlined in this book and in *Innovative Games* (Lichtman, 1993) are designed to meet this instructional challenge.

However, when masses must share the same facility during inclement weather, games played in areas that most do not consider typical can ease the burden of overcrowding. Specifically, halls, corners, out-of-bounds portions of courts, stairwells, and outside walls meet those requirements. Two approaches may be employed when using such spaces to develop games. The first requires modifying the rules and actions of a standard activity to fit within the confines of the existing space. This demands less abstraction than the second approach, where one develops a unique game to fit within that locale. Regardless of which process is employed, the creation should be innovative.

Consider the different qualities each area could provide. Halls and corners are especially adapted for permitting balls to rebound from walls at uncommon angles. Halls, because of their marbled or tiled floors, allow smooth objects to slide. Abundant exterior windowless wall space generally exists at most schools or recreational centers. Because of its unimpeded height, many activities requiring a large area from which balls ricochet can be accommodated. Once one activity is adapted or developed for an underutilized locale, generally other games may be created merely by substituting other equipment or by infusing different motor skills. Participants do not see activities such as racquetball and handball as similar; therefore it is unlikely that they will recognize the similarity between the hallway versions of paddleball and two-square.

The Games

The activities in this chapter are grouped first by the locale in which they are played, then further arranged according to the ease with which most individuals can execute the needed motor skills. When attempting to judge the difficulty of games at the same site, the speed with which participants must react and the familiarity with the equipment are variables that must be considered. Additionally, since an understanding and integration of angles of incidence and refraction is required, the ability of participants to incorporate this mechanical principle within their motor actions is another factor. Any hall activity where use of the non-preferred hand is demanded increases the difficulty. While doubles play increases cooperative demands, generally it is considered less difficult, as ability to cover the court doesn't pose a problem. However, three-armed action where the middle arms of two players are joined together is definitely the most difficult.

REBOUND BOWLING

Requiring players to roll, kick, or strike a ball with a hockey stick or baseball bat so that it must ricochet off walls in a designated pattern before any pins may be knocked down increases the challenge found in traditional bowling.

Objectives

Reinforces kicking, throwing, batting, and ball rolling skills. Reviews scoring used in bowling and enhances knowledge of rebound angles.

Equipment

Ten bowling pins or Indian clubs, and one soccer ball or volleyball per alley. Depending on the actions specified, one bat and one hockey stick. If foul lanes are desired, two polyspots or tape can be used. One bowling score sheet, with the exact requirements enumerated for each shot, and one pencil per alley.

Playing Area

Each court requires a hall that is 30 to 45 feet (9.1 to 13.7 meters) long and 8 to 16 feet (2.4 to 4.9 meters) wide. The lower 2 feet (0.6 meter) of wall area should be free of obstructions.

Participants

Up to four players per alley.

Game

Pins are set up as in traditional bowling; however, they are centered with respect to the sidewalls. To help position the pins properly, a small piece of tape may be affixed to the floor where the 1, 7, and 10 pins would normally stand. Pre-designed trajectory and motor skill requirements for each ball in each frame are determined, and specified on the score sheets, as seen in figure 9.1, which depicts actions required during only the first five frames. Vary the actions to increase the complexity and challenge beyond those typically demanded in standard bowling. A list of possibilities follows.

Frame	*First Ball*	*Second Ball*
1	Back Facing Two-Hand Roll	Kick Off Right Sidewall
2	One-Hand Roll Off Left Sidewall	Heel Kick
3	Two-Hand Roll Off Right Sidewall	Back Facing One-Hand Roll Off Left Sidewall
4	Kick Off Left Sidewall, Rebound From Right Sidewall	Left-Hand Roll Off Right Sidewall
5	Back Facing Two-Hand Roll	Left-Foot Kick Off Left Sidewall

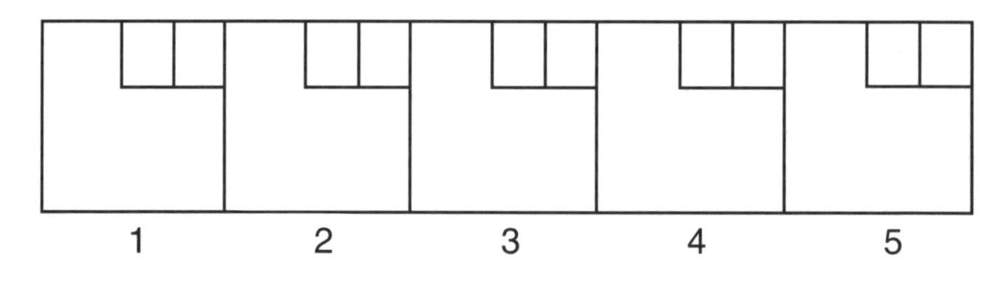

Note: The requirements for the frames appear on page 149

Figure 9.1 Score sheet and trajectory requirements during first five frames.

The movements may be expanded by requiring delivery with the left hand, right hand, left foot, or right foot. Also included are shots that do not demand contact with the walls prior to toppling the pins (figure 9.2).

- Using a one- or two-hand roll, a kick, or striking action with a hockey stick or bat,
    a. send ball directly to the pins;
    b. propel ball to left sidewall, contacting the pins from the rebound; or

Figure 9.2 Frame one first ball action from Rebound Bowling showing a Back Facing Two-Hand Roll.

c. propel ball to right sidewall, contacting the pins from the rebound (figure 9.3).

- With your back to the pins or a sidewall and using a one- or two-handed roll or one-heel kick,
  a. send ball directly to the pins;
  b. propel ball to left sidewall, contacting the pins from the rebound; or
  c. propel ball to the right sidewall, contacting the pins from the rebound.
- Using a one- or two-handed roll, kick, or striking action with a hockey stick or bat, send ball off one wall so that it ricochets from the other wall and contacts the pins directly from that rebound.
- If pins are set up 8 to 10 feet (2.4 to 3.0 meters) in front of an endwall, use a one- or two-handed toss, punt, or a drop kick to propel the ball so it rebounds from the end wall and directly contacts the pins.

Figure 9.3 Frame one second ball action from Rebound Bowling showing a kick off the right sidewall.

HALLBALL THREE WAYS

The racket/paddle variation melds a netless version of table tennis with the ability to hit balls to the side walls, creating a game that is similar to racquetball but without a front or back wall. With hitting implements eliminated, a handball modification emerges.

Objectives

Develops propulsion skills and the ability to make decisions quickly, integrates knowledge of rebound angles, and stresses anticipatory reaction speed. The hand version improves ambidextrous actions, especially when played with a small-sized ball.

Equipment

Racket/Paddle Version: two pickleball or table tennis paddles, one tennis ball or racquetball, and six polyspots per court. Handball Version: one tennis ball, racquetball, or volleyball, and six polyspots per court.

Playing Area

Hallways 7 to 10 feet (2.1 to 3.0 meters) wide are suited to singles or three-armed style play, while those 10 to 16 feet (3.0 to 4.9 meters) wide are used for doubles action. For halls wider than 10 feet (3.0 meters) or where a different version of singles play is desired, consult the Helpful Hints section for modifications to a one-sidewalled court. Total court length varies between 10 and 18 feet (3.0 and 5.5 meters) depending on the type of game, style of play, and equipment used. Generally a longer court is required for doubles play, when using rackets/paddles, or if using balls with greater rebound properties. Minimally, the lower five feet (1.5 meters) of the sidewalls should be free from obstructions and relatively smooth. Polyspots are placed along the juncture of the sidewalls and the corners of the two boxes that define the court. If possible place spots on a line formed by the pieces of marble or tile. This will assist players in judging balls that are out-of-bounds. Figure 9.4 depicts the typical court layout.

Participants

Singles play requires two players; doubles and three-armed action involves four players per court.

Game

The following rules pertain to all versions of Hallball. Points are begun using an underhand serve that is contacted after the server drops the ball in her box. The server must contact the ball below waist and wrist level. The ball must first bounce in the opponent's half of the court, and

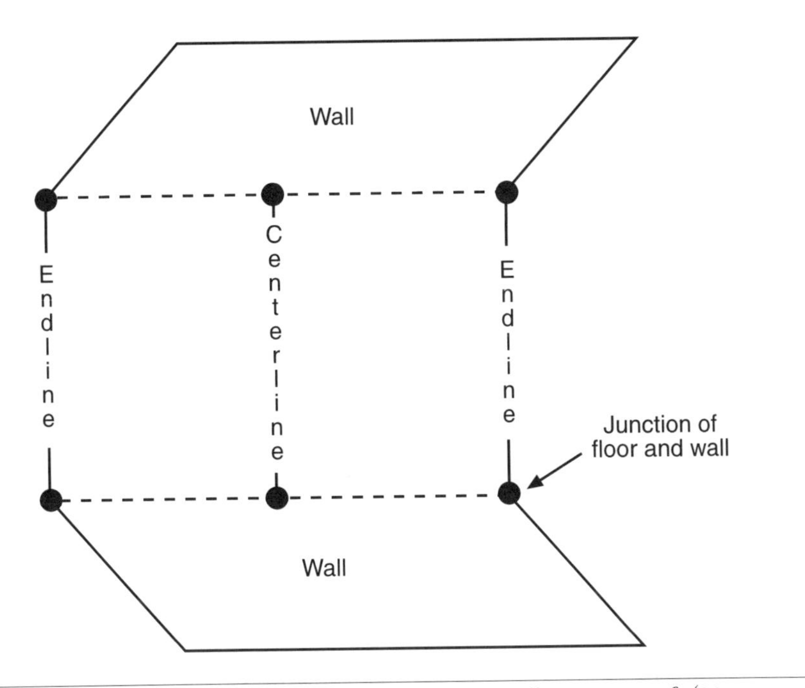

Figure 9.4 Hallball court design used for narrow hallways 7 to 10 ft (2.1 to 3.0 m) wide.

the trajectory of the serve must be such that if the opponent purposely chooses to let the ball go, it would not hit a sidewall prior to contacting the floor a second time. Additionally, the ball must rebound from the floor to a minimum of mid-thigh height. This is to prevent individuals from serving the ball so forcefully that it results in an automatic ace.

Once the serve is delivered, players are permitted to have one foot in the box they are defending. During a rally, players may contact the ball using any valid volleyball technique. For each hit thereafter, the ball must be returned either directly or after hitting one or both sidewalls so that the first bounce on the floor is within the opponent's half of the court. Note, balls contacting the sidewall may hit the portion over either half of the court. Legal contacts may be made from either a volley or after a single bounce. Fifteen points defines a game provided that a player is ahead by two points. Points can be earned only while serving. Should a player have both of his feet across the endline of his half of the court or should a double hit occur (the player contacts the ball twice consecutively) a side-out or point is awarded.

For doubles play, the server has the option of sending the ball toward either opponent. The serving order and rotation after a point is made is identical to badminton. Other than these modifications, other rules stated above pertain. Figure 9.5 shows Hallball doubles using a volleyball.

Figure 9.5 Hallball action on a two-walled court using a volleyball.

In the three-armed version, players hold inner hands, and similar rules apply. However, when a beachball is used, the server may deliver the ball without it first having to bounce on the floor, and the serve only has to rebound to knee level. If a foam-type soccer-sized ball is used, the server puts the ball in play after it rebounds from the floor. When a point is gained, the serving partners change the hand each is grasping to require the server to use the opposite hand. Note, for less highly skilled players, rather than changing positions after each point is earned, switch after the other team has lost its service. A ball that is struck by the joined middle hands is considered to be a single contact. Partners may form a standard volleyball bumping position, if they interlace their fingers and extend their thumbs. Each person in the twosome is permitted to have one foot in the box.

Safety Considerations

Doubles competition with rackets or paddles could result in one player inadvertently contacting another, especially if players do not agree ahead of time on who is responsible for shots sent down the center of the court. Typically, the player with the forehand stroke covers that area.

Helpful Hints

Players often think they gain an advantage by hitting the ball with tremendous force. Occasionally this might be successful, but a strategy focusing on placement and finesse is more effective. To avoid a smash as a return, contact the ball so it doesn't result in a high rebound. If you can aim the ball at your opponent's foot before that person is able to step back, it will force him to return the shot with a difficult half-volley stroke. In the hand version, be sure to allow practice with the non-preferred hand prior to game play.

A unique version of singles play may be introduced or would be required for hallways wider than 10 feet (3.0 meters) by modifying the court to use only one sidewall, as shown in figure 9.6. The female player is in the traditional defensive position, close to where the side- and endline meet, to protect for shots that rebound from the wall on a very shallow angle.

A player is permitted only one foot in the box, but entry could take place by stepping over the line running parallel with the wall, as the male has done, or from the other direction. The action in single-walled play is far more demanding and should be reserved for advanced players only. Strategy suggests that one try to get his opponent out of position by varying hits that are sent straight into the competitor's box with those that first rebound from the sidewall.

Figure 9.6 Hallball court in wide hallway. The girl is in a standard defensive position while the boy has assumed a more offensive location.

Adaptations for Younger Participants

For younger or less highly skilled players, consider using a small-sized utility ball, a high-density foam ball that bounces readily, or even small- to medium-sized beachballs.

ONE-WALLED VOLLEYBALL

In a limited space, elements of singles or doubles handball are blended with volleyball skills to create an exciting activity in which players attempt to send the ball to a wall in such a way that the opposing team is unable to return the ball before it bounces twice.

Objectives

Reinforces all volleyball actions except overhand serving. Enhances agility and teamwork.

Equipment

One volleyball and a minimum of eight polyspots per court. Tape or chalk for placing lines on the wall.

Playing Area

An unobstructed and relatively smooth wall at least 10 feet (3.0 meters) high with an adjoining floor or concrete space measuring 15 to 20 feet (4.6 to 6.1 meters) by 25 to 30 feet (7.6 to 9.1 meters). The court dimensions shown in figure 9.7 are geared for ages 13 and beyond where a volleyball is used. One-Walled Volleyball may also be played on a tennis court that possesses a backboard; however, this facility is not as desirable as a wooden surface reduces the rebound effect when a volleyball is used.

Many gymnasiums are already marked with lines that form the back alleys of a badminton court. These lines may be used to form the serving zone. If the painted lines are not positioned appropriately, then mark a line with polyspots to define the service zone.

Participants

Two to four players per court.

Game

The flow of the game is much the same as in one-walled handball, with 15 points equaling a game provided a two-point difference exists. Points can be gained only while serving. Only one chance is provided to deliver an underhand serve that contacts the wall on a fly above the three-foot

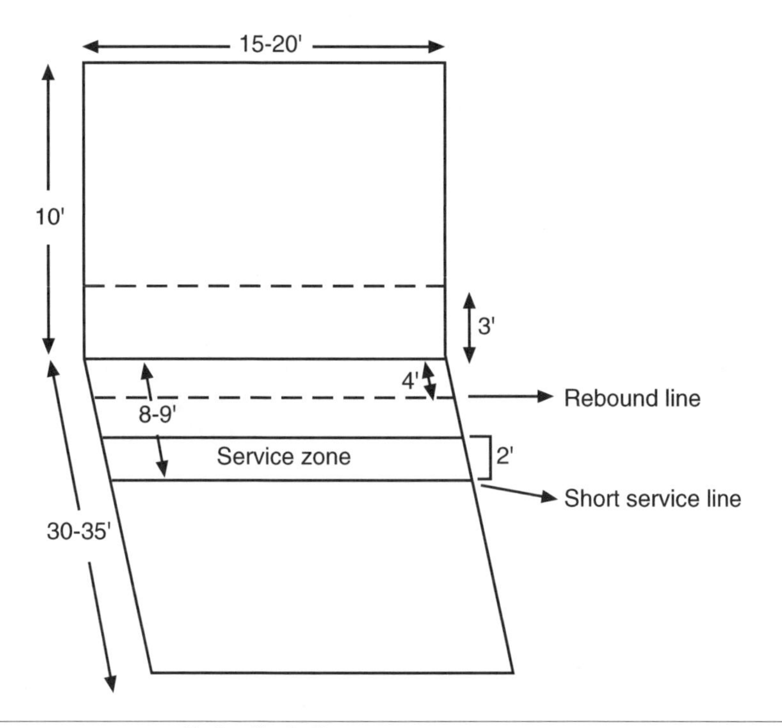

Figure 9.7 One-Walled Volleyball court setup.

(0.9-meter) line, passes the short service line, and bounces in bounds. In doubles play both members of the serving team must be within the service zone or must have at least one foot in contact with the short service line and may not move from that locale until the ball has passed the short service line. One-Walled Volleyball uses the same rotational serving pattern as racquetball. During a rally players may either contact the ball after a single bounce or on a volley, and the initial bounce after hitting the wall must occur beyond the four-foot (1.2-meter) rebound line that is parallel to the short service line. Both players from a team do not have to contact the ball prior to it traveling to the wall. The ball is permitted to bounce only once between successive contacts.

After the return of the serve, a teammate may opt to pass the ball to her partner provided she yells "set" prior to her contact. In that instance, the ball is only allowed to bounce on the playing surface a maximum of one time before it is returned to the front wall. In other words, three possible execution patterns are legal for the team trying to return the ball when each partner will be involved in the return:

- Bounce from front wall, hitter #1 announces "set" and volleys the ball to hitter #2, who sends the ball directly to the front wall (note, no bounce occurred between the partners' contacts).

- Hitter #1 yells "set" and contacts the ball from the wall before it bounces; hitter #2 lets the ball bounce once (note, this bounce must be within the court) prior to sending it to the front wall.
- The same as the instance immediately above, except that hitter #2 opts to contact the ball directly from hitter #1's volley.

The setting option does not exist in singles play.

Players are responsible for calling their own carries or double hits. Additionally, opponents must allow the opposing team members an opportunity to play the ball while unimpeded, or else a hinder is called and the point is replayed. Should an opponent be hit by the ball while it is traveling toward the wall, the point is replayed only if there was a reasonable chance that the ball would have made it to the wall on a fly and hit above the three-foot (0.9-meter) line. During a rally, it is legal to play the ball while standing out-of-bounds.

Safety Considerations

In doubles, encourage players to call for the ball and communicate with each other, especially when one individual wants to set for another. The defense should avoid the temptation to turn and watch opponents contact the ball even though the chance of being hit is fairly small. Occasionally a player will intentionally hinder an opponent by sliding in front of the hitter as a spike is just about to be delivered. This action is dangerous for both players and should be penalized by adding one or two points to the team that was attempting to hit the ball. Congestion when moving from the frontcourt to the backcourt, or vice versa, may be avoided by going toward or outside the sidelines. Leave at least six to seven feet (1.8 to 2.1 meters) between courts.

Helpful Hints

Effective serves and returns force opponents to hit the ball from deep within the court. For doubles play, once the serve passes the short service line, players should either play a side-by-side, up-and-back, or rotational strategy. With the side-by-side technique, teammates should try to position themselves in the middle of the court, forcing opponents to play deeper. When using an up-and-back approach, the forecourt player is responsible for balls that land between the wall and within five feet (1.5 meters) in back of the short service line. The rotational method is the most advanced. Here, if an offensive-type return is delivered, the player hitting that shot generally moves to the front position, while the partner locates himself further back in the court. However, if a defensive return results, with an opposing player setting or about to deliver a spike, then opponents assume a side-by-side positioning toward the back third of the court.

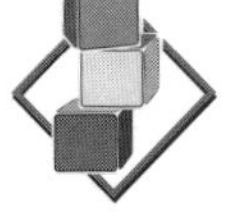

Adaptations for Younger Participants

For less highly skilled players, a foam volleyball or a beachball can be used. If a beachball is substituted, players as young as fourth grade can compete, provided they have received some preliminary instruction. For fifth and sixth graders, or where a foam ball will be used, reduce court width by about 3 feet (0.9 meter) and length by 4 to 6 feet (1.2 to 1.8 meters). When using a beachball, court width is the same as the court dimensions seen in figure 9.7, but the length is decreased by 8 to 10 feet (2.4 to 3.0 meters), and the short service line is moved to within 5 or 6 feet (1.5 or 1.8 meters) of the wall.

CORNER BALL

Players try to hit a ball to a wall so that it rebounds into the opponent's court and can't be returned using a maximum of two consecutive hits with no more than one bounce between contacts.

Objectives

Develops bilateral hand striking patterns and split second decision making.

Equipment

Tape and one racquetball per court.

Playing Area

Any unobstructed corner where a 6.5-foot (2.0-meter) square can be taped, with two of the sides being formed by the junction of the floor and the walls. See figure 9.8 for a diagram of the court.

Participants

Two per court.

Game

Using an underhand serve from a dropped ball, a player must send the ball so that it bounces from the opponent's portion of the wall directly into the opponent's floor space. Thereafter, the ball must be returned using no more than two consecutive contacts such that after hitting any one or two walls, without restriction as to whose wall space is hit or hit first, the ball bounces back into the server's floor space. Should the ball rebound from a wall into the opponent's half of the court without the need for a second successive contact, the opponent must play the ball. Rallying continues, using these requirements, until one of the following occurs:

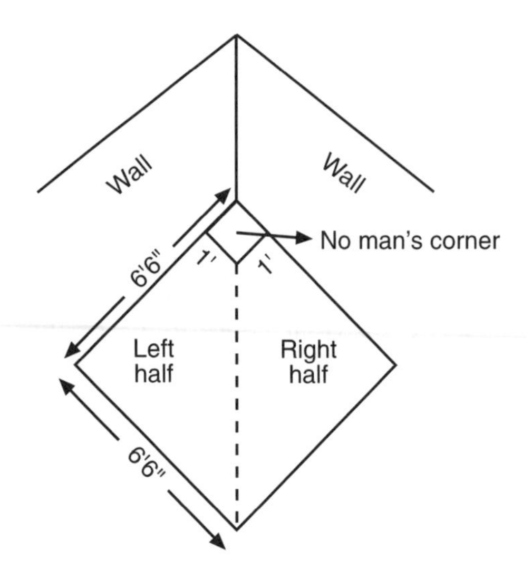

Figure 9.8 Corner Ball court layout.

- The ball bounces out of the taped playing area.
- A ball bounces in the no-man's corner.
- A player crosses into the court with more than one foot.
- From a contact, the ball hits the floor before the wall.

In each of the above cases, the player committing the violation is at fault, resulting in a side-out or point. Points can be gained only while serving. After each earned point, players change halves of the court alternating the areas they will serve to and defend. Fifteen points make up a game, as long as at least a two-point difference exists. The first server is determined arbitrarily. The opening serve of the game is delivered from the playing position on the right side of the court. If one player interferes with another, the point is replayed. A ball which lands on the line dividing the two halves of the floor space is considered good. Thus, should a ball be hit by player #1 and land on that dividing line, player #2 would have to return the ball.

Helpful Hints

This game is much more difficult than it appears. Initial practice should be given to let players individually learn how the ball will react when rebounding off each wall and two walls. Players will quickly learn that this is not a game of power but rather demands finesse and the ability to deliver a controlled stroke using either hand.

10

Developing Multi-Principled Creations

This book introduces, discusses, and provides examples of the seven principles for developing innovative games. While each can be used independently, there is no logical reason to prevent the amalgamation of two or more tenets into a single activity or the further generalization of one principle beyond the scope of its original presentation. In fact, application of such a process would provide limitless possibilities! Novel activities previously presented under a single principle can now incorporate elements from a second principle. While these creations might initially appear to adults to be extensions of the original activity, in most instances youngsters will perceive them as different games. This can be approached from the more abstract by working with the principles themselves or by employing a more straightforward strategy through adopting the idea suggested in chapter 3, Developing Hybrid Activities. Common sports are placed on the horizontal axis while selected novel activities which appear from different principles, presented in this book and in *Innovative Games* (Lichtman, 1993), or in other resources, are situated along the vertical axis as seen in table 10.1. When common sports are listed, be certain that they do not appear in both axes, as that would result in the development of hybrid games seen in chapter 3.

It seems obvious that not all integrations could work, and some care must be exercised in selecting exactly which games should serve as the springboards for melding together. If merging seems possible, then be prepared to further adapt where necessary. In many cases, this will require developing new rules, using a different player configuration, or moving the activity to a location different from that of the games in which the emerging product is rooted. While the examples above provide only mixtures from two novel activities, adding a third alternative to the conglomeration might result in a more effective creation.

Table 10.1

Schema for Developing Multi-Principled Novel Activities Using Existing Innovative Games Themselves, or Combined With Standard Sports

	INNOVATIVE GAME (PRINCIPLE)	
Standard sport	**Mazeball* (changing goal or player setup)**	**Pole Foosball**** (multimedia adaptation)**
Basketball	Basket-Mazeball**	Foosball Kaleidoscope**
Volleyball	Volley-Mazeball***	Volley-Foosball***

*Based on data from *Innovative Games* (Lichtman, 1993, pp. 65-68).

**These activities appear in this chapter.

***A special section has been added to the basketball versions of each of these games which briefly describes how the action could be extended to include the volleyball variation. The information provided does not give as in-depth an explanation as the two games from which these other activities have been developed.

****From chapter 8, pp. 132-136.

The Games

The games are arranged according to the number of participants that can be accommodated on one court or field, with the activity involving the largest group appearing last.

RICOCHET FUNGO SOFTBALL

Players compete individually by hitting a tennis ball fungo-style against a wall, while three other players, against whom the batter is competing, attempt to catch the ball on the fly and record an out. If the ball bounces, a hit is recorded depending upon how far the distance is from the wall before a defensive player can control the ball. After each hit, the batter immediately runs to a receptacle to get another ball and returns to the hitter's box before hitting again. Once a player gains control, the ball must be returned to the box. If at any point no balls are in the receptacle, the batter is awarded three extra runs. Each hitter's at bat lasts a total of four minutes or three outs, whichever comes first.

Objectives

Develops hitting, fielding, and throwing skills while rewarding speed and agility.

Equipment

For each game, three tennis balls, one bat, four cones (unless the activity is played on a tennis court), chalk to designate a batter's box, a stopwatch, and a small box or receptacle to hold the tennis balls. Note, depending on the strength and skill of the batters, old tennis balls might be required if players can consistently hit balls beyond the deepest part of the playing area, or racquetballs may be used if longer trajectories are needed.

Playing Area

A windowless wall that is at least 15 to 20 feet (4.6 to 6.1 meters) high, preferably made of concrete. An unobstructed area that is 35 to 40 feet (10.7 to 12.2 meters) wide and extends at least 110 feet (33.5 meters) from the wall. Figure 10.1 shows the setup for this type of playing area.

Note, if special care is taken, this game may be played on a tennis court if backboards are available. Figure 10.2 displays the court setup for play on a tennis court. The boundaries on a tennis court are defined by the doubles sidelines, which theoretically extend back to the fence.

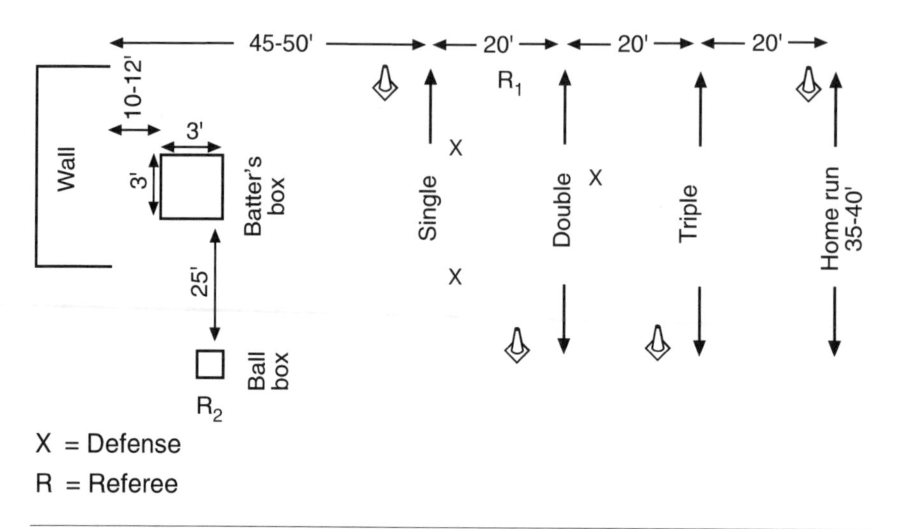

Figure 10.1 Ricochet Fungo Softball field design and player setup when played against a concrete wall.

Participants

Six people per court. Two serve as referees, one is the batter, and the remaining three are fielders.

Game

The game begins with the three fielders on the opposite side of the net, referee #1 located by the net post furthest from the ball box, referee #2 positioned near the ball box, and the batter in the batter's box with a ball in hand. When time begins, the batter fungo-hits the ball so that it rebounds from the backboard and is sent over the net.

A strike occurs if the batter fails to make contact, swings while out of the batter's box, or fails to hit the ball beyond the serving area. Two consecutive strikes equal an out. An out also occurs if the ball is caught on the fly within the playing area. An out is also called if the ball is hit so that the first bounce occurs out-of-bounds, provided the ball was not touched by a fielder.

If the ball lands within fair territory, advancement by an imaginary base runner takes place. The number of bases earned is dictated by the section of the playing area in which ball control was achieved:

A single—from the service line to the net.

A double—from net to the service line on the other side of the net.

A triple—from the service line to the baseline on the other side of the net.

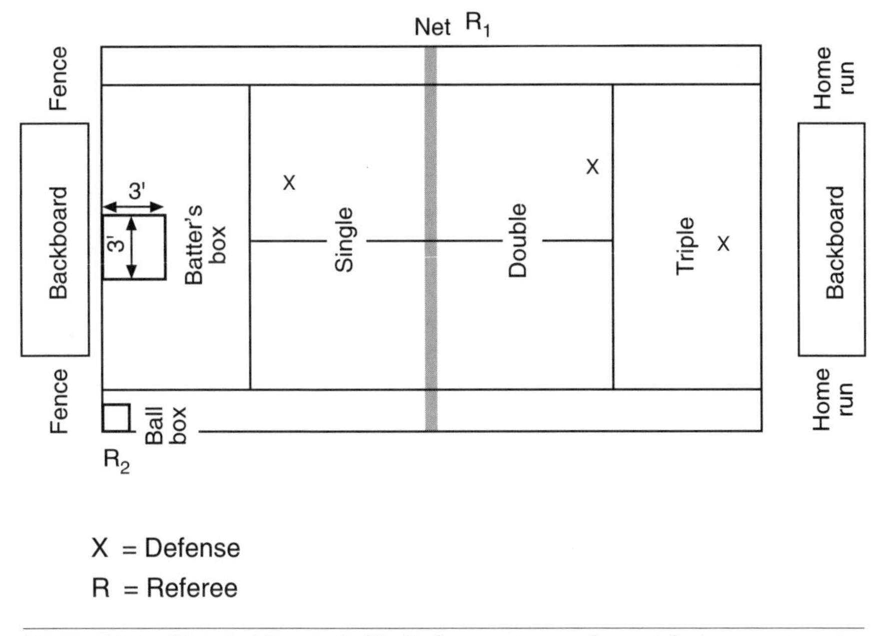

Figure 10.2 Ricochet Fungo Softball player setup and court design on a tennis court.

A home run—the ball hits the fence or opposite backboard, either on the fly or on the bounce.

If a strike occurs, the batter must secure that ball and return to the batter's box to fungo-hit again. If the ball went over the net and landed out-of-bounds prior to a fielder touching the ball, time stops and the action ceases until that ball is returned to the batter. Should the batter already have another ball in her hand, one is returned to the ball box. The watch is restarted when the batter is positioned in the batter's box and ready to hit another ball.

If the ball goes into the playing area, the hitter should run as quickly as possible to the ball box, get another ball, return to the batter's box, and hit again (figure 10.3). While this is occurring, once a member of the fielding team catches the ball on a fly or otherwise gains control of it, the ball should be returned to the ball box as quickly as possible. Two balls may be returned at the same time, but there is a far greater risk that the batter will have sent the third ball into fair territory before the other balls are returned to the receptacle and the three-run penalty will apply.

While the hitter is trying to score as many runs as possible within the four minutes, she is also attempting to create a situation where the ball

Figure 10.3 Rushing to return a ball to the ball box in Ricochet Fungo Softball. The hitter wastes no time in putting another ball in play, trying to catch the defense off guard, and hoping to empty the ball box to gain three extra runs.

box is empty to earn an additional three runs. Fielders are trying to gain outs and prevent imaginary runners from further advancement while ensuring that at least one ball is always in the ball box. An effective strategy is for the fielder who caught or initially gained control of the ball to toss the ball to a second fielder, who is now near the ball box, while quickly getting into position to play the next fungo hit. If the ball box becomes empty, time stops and all balls are returned to the ball box. The watch is restarted when the fungo hitter in the batter's box has a ball in hand.

Referee #1 is in charge of calling out the result of each fungo contact and follows what is occurring with the imaginary base runners and the number of runs that have been scored. Referee #2 keeps track of the number of strikes, outs, balls in the box, and time. After four minutes have elapsed, or three outs, whichever comes first, players rotate in the following order: referee #1 becomes the batter; the batter assumes fielder #1's position; fielder #1 takes over for referee #2; referee #2 moves to fielder #2's spot; fielder #2 takes over for fielder #3; and fielder #3 moves into the role of referee #1.

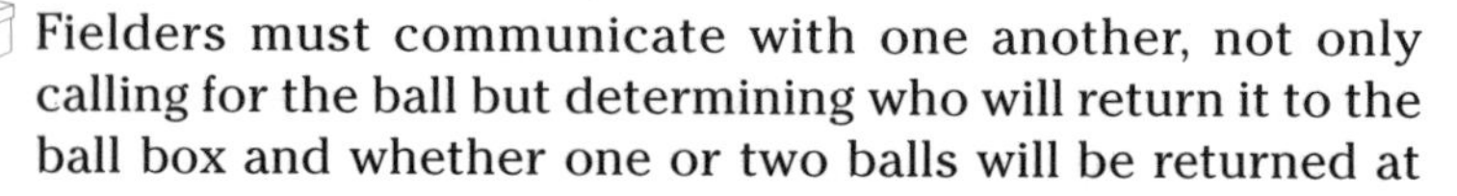

Safety Considerations

Fielders must communicate with one another, not only calling for the ball but determining who will return it to the ball box and whether one or two balls will be returned at once. It is possible for a fielder who is playing the ball to be hit by another ball after it rebounds from the bat or from the backboard, but the chance is very small. While the net serves as an obstacle, it usually does not cause problems for the fielders. If concern exists about a fielder getting hurt by running into the net, establish a ground rule that prohibits a defender from reaching over the net to catch a fly.

Helpful Hints

Participants should possess the ability to fungo-hit before this activity is attempted. If players have difficulty, this activity may be played using a tennis racket instead of a bat, livelier tennis balls or racquetballs, or the batter's box may be moved closer to the backboard. Generally, players will need to hit the ball fairly high on the backboard to provide a steep enough angle of trajectory to allow the ball to travel beyond the net. If players have difficulty with imaginary base runners, simply convert the scoring areas to points rather than bases earned.

Adaptations for Younger Participants

Options discussed in the Helpful Hints section can be tried. If these are not successful, then consider the following additional alternatives:

1. Use a racquetball to have players throw at the backboard.
2. Reconfigure the awarding of bases as follows (with this court design, one or two fielders should play in front of the net):
    - A single—from the service line on the hitter's/thrower's side of the net to the net.
    - A double—the ball rolls into the net.
    - A triple—over the net to the service line.
    - Home run—over the net and beyond the service line.
3. Using a tennis ball, yarn ball, or Wiffle ball, with the original court design, have the hitter/thrower stand near the backboard facing the opposite side of the court and swing at or throw the ball. The exact modification will depend upon the skill level and power of the participants.
4. All of the scoring areas should be moved so that they are beyond the net. For example: net to service line, one point; service line to baseline, two points; baseline to backboard, three points; on fly to opposite backboard, four points.

SOFT-VOLLEY-SOCCER

Integrate volleyball with soccer skills, place within a modified softball-type setting, and a "tribrid" activity emerges where the goal is to earn more runs than your opponents but within a context that provides greater challenge and an enhanced variety of motor actions.

Objectives

Develops soccer, volleyball, and batting skills, and reinforces most softball rules.

Equipment

One baseball bat, five bases, one home plate, one old volleyball, one floor hockey-size net, or a net of similar size. If players lack the ability to "toss" the ball with reasonable accuracy to the batter, a batting tee may be used.

Playing Area

A softball field or grassy area where the bases, home plate, and the net can be set up. Figure 10.4 shows the configuration of the field.

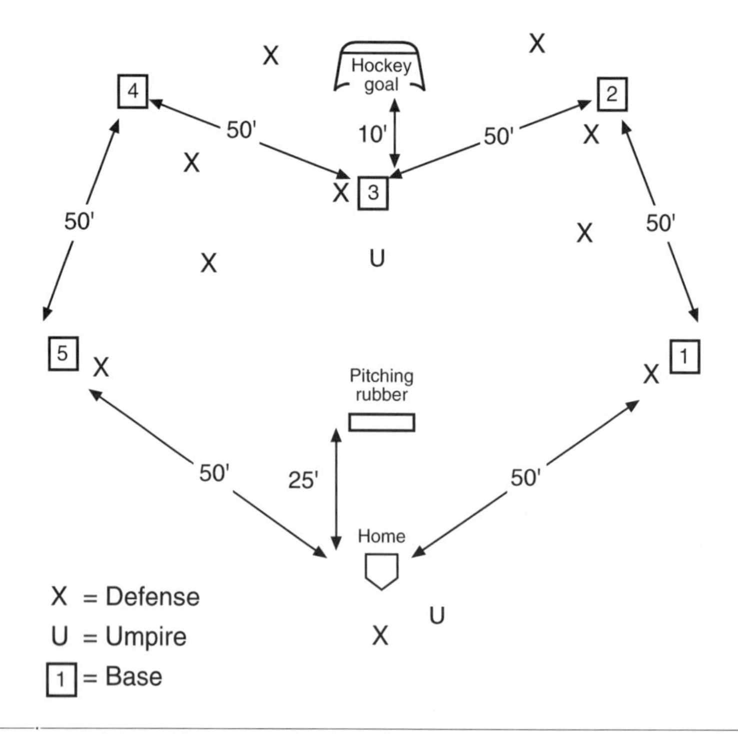

Figure 10.4 Soft-Volley-Soccer field configuration and player setup.

Participants

Nine to 11 players per team (one pitcher, one catcher, five basemen, one to two goalies/outfielders, and two to three additional infielders) and two umpires.

Game

Offensive play follows standard slow-pitch softball action, except that two additional bases must be touched and players must skip when traversing from base to base. Furthermore, since there are no base paths between adjacent bases (first and second, second and third, and so on), skippers may take any path they desire so long as the bases are traversed in the proper order.

If a pitcher is used, the ball must be tossed with a high arc similar to that required in slow-pitch softball. When playing the ball, fielders must adhere to the following requirements: if the ball rebounds directly from the playing surface, it must be played with the feet. If the ball rebounds directly from the bat or part of a fielder's body, the ball may be caught or played on the fly using any volleyball or soccer technique, except those involving throwing. Thus, the only time the ball is permitted to be thrown or tossed while in play is when the ball is pitched. When a ball is caught, the player who secured the ball may take no more than three steps.

Each time a new batter/base skipper hits the ball in play, the fielding team is allowed to complete a maximum of two catches prior to termination of the play by

- an out,
- return of the ball to the pitcher within the pitcher's circle, or
- sending of the ball into the goal.

Attempted but unsuccessful catches do not count against the two-catch rule.

An out occurs when

- a second strike is earned,
- a batted ball is caught on the fly,
- the ball arrives at first base or in the goal before the base skipper can reach first base, or the lead skipper who is being forced can't arrive at the base he is trying to reach (in this last case, the lead skipper is out),
- the ball arrives at any base where there is a force before the skipper can get there,
- the base skipper is hit at or below the waist by a ball that has been played using a volleyball or soccer technique,

- a skipper is tagged while off base, or
- a base skipper uses a running action.

Lifting or carrying when executing a volleyball skill is not called unless it was an obvious attempt to push or almost throw the ball. Additionally, as in the traditional game of volleyball, a player is not permitted to use a volleyball technique to contact the ball two or more times consecutively. Note, it would be legal for a fielder to kick the ball to himself, immediately play the ball using a volleyball technique, then catch the ball, and finally serve it to another player. In this example, the catch separates the two volleyball contacts so they were not consecutive.

The possibility for multiple outs occurs if, after the ball is hit into fair territory and prior to the ball being touched by a second fielder, the pitcher or a designated player yells "netball." Once "netball" is called, the ball must be played into the goal, as any other type of action, including being hit or tagged out, has no affect upon the runners. During a "netball" play, an umpire should blow a whistle to signal when the ball arrives in the goal. Any skipper who is not on a base when the whistle blows is automatically out.

If the pitcher or designated player does not call "netball" and the ball is sent into the net, the only players that could be out are the skipper, who is trying to get to first if there are no other forces, or the lead skipper, who is being forced. All other skippers automatically advance to the base they were trying to reach. Violation of any fielding rules stops play, awarding to all skippers the base toward which they were heading plus an extra base.

Safety Considerations

If an underhand volleyball serve is used, instruct fielders that to hit base runners at or below waist level, they will need to send the ball on a very flat trajectory to prevent the ball from rising too high. This is accomplished by bending at the waist and striking more toward the middle of the ball's surface facing the hitter, rather than underneath the ball.

Helpful Hints

If defensive skills are not developed enough to offset skipping speed, require that skippers circle each base or plate once or twice before they may head to the next base. Initially players will have a tendency to field ground balls with their hands unless reminded just prior to each new batter. It also is of help if a player, usually the pitcher, or an umpire keeps track of and calls out the number of catches that have occurred during the action for each new batter/base skipper. Prior to allowing "netball" plays, be sure that participants are well versed in the basic rules. Strategy dictates forcing fielders to play the ball with their feet by hitting ground balls. Fielders should realize that it will be much harder to get a runner out at a base if the two catches have already been used for a new base skipper.

Adaptations for Younger Participants

Use a batting tee in place of a pitcher. Be sure participants have developed the skill to loft the ball to themselves using their feet. Until players are comfortable with the fielding rules, do not use the hockey net, thus eliminating this option for earning outs. Once individuals are familiar with the flow of the game, introduce the net, but do not allow "netball" plays until players have become accustomed to using the goal as another means to score an out.

FOOSBALL KALEIDOSCOPE

Applying the concept from the table game version of alternating lines of players from opposing teams to perform a combination of actions from basketball, team handball, and soccer results in a fast moving activity in which players are given three options for scoring.

Objectives

Reinforces selected skills from soccer, volleyball, and basketball.

Equipment

Two to four soft soccer- or volleyball-sized balls, 12 to 20 pinnies, 20 polyspots, and masking tape.

Playing Area

A basketball court where walls are located within 9 to 15 feet (2.7 to 4.6 meters) of the endlines. If a natural boundary exists within a few feet of the sidelines, such as a wall or curtain, the playing area is extended to include those structures.

Participants

Twelve to 20 per team, with each team divided into four different lines as shown in figure 10.5, which depicts the court setup and player configuration. Two referees are needed if two balls are used. If a third or fourth ball is included, four referees should be employed, with each responsible for one-quarter of the playing area.

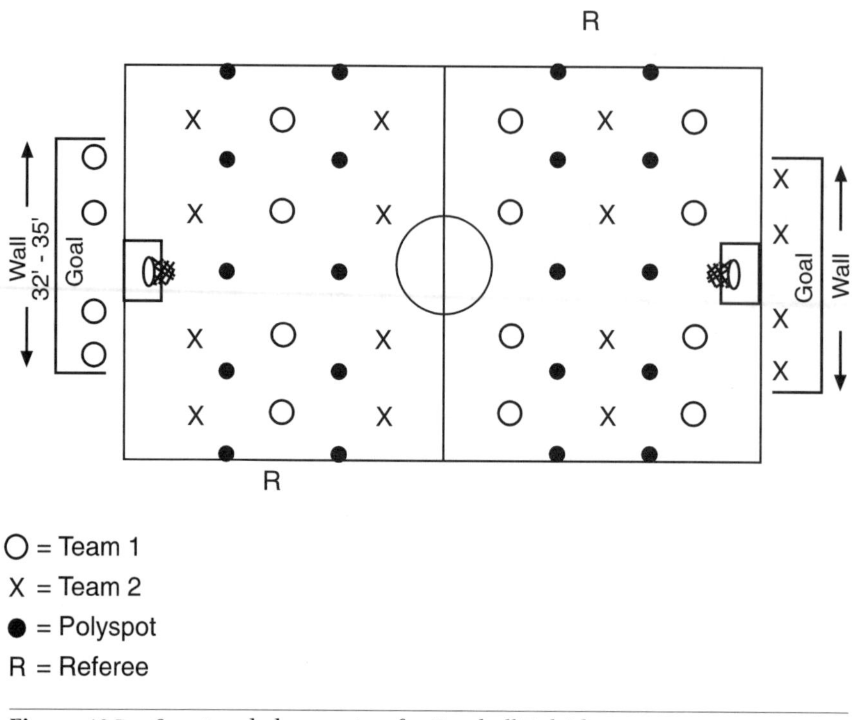

Figure 10.5 Court and player setup for Foosball Kaleidoscope.

Game

The following rules dictate how specific lines of participants are permitted to play the ball, as well as their general responsibilities. *Goalies:* Prevent opposing teams from scoring into goals taped on the endwalls and may use any part of their bodies to defend the goal but must have both feet behind the endline. *Court Players:* Each line of players must stay within its third of the half of the court in which they are positioned. *Outermost Two Lines of Court Players:* These participants may not use their hands to play the ball unless they are facing the goalies and are trying to block a pass from a goalie. Should any outermost player catch a goalie pass, the ball must be dropped immediately, and play continues, using feet. *Inner Four Lines of Court Players:* These individuals may use their hands and feet to play the ball but are not permitted to use their hands to play a ball that rebounds directly from the floor. Thus, the ball must be tipped up to oneself or to another player with the feet before hands may be used. Every time points are scored, the ball is given to one of the goalies who was just scored upon and play continues. If a ball hits the endwall but does not result in a goal, the ball is still considered in play. Violations by goalies while an opponent is in the act of shooting into the endwall goal result in an automatic score. Violations by a court player result in the nearest opposing line gaining possession of the ball. If one of the members of the inner four lines is given the ball, she is permitted to play the ball with her hands to initiate this change of possession.

The game begins with one ball given to each line of goalies. If a third or fourth ball is added, one of the referees should roll both balls into play near midcourt after the other two balls have been put into play. On the whistle, play continues nonstop for five rounds, each lasting four to five minutes. After each round, players change positions. Goalies switch to court player positions on the same half they were defending. The middle line of court players on one side crosses midcourt to become the line of court players nearest the centerline on their offensive half. Players who were closest to midcourt move to the line in front of the goal they will be shooting for, while those who were positioned in the line immediately in front of the opposing team's goalies assume the position of their team's goalies. (Figure 10.6 shows a schematic of the line shifts.)

Points are earned when goals are made in the following ways:

- Taped Goals: A kicked ball is awarded two points; a ball that is thrown earns one point.

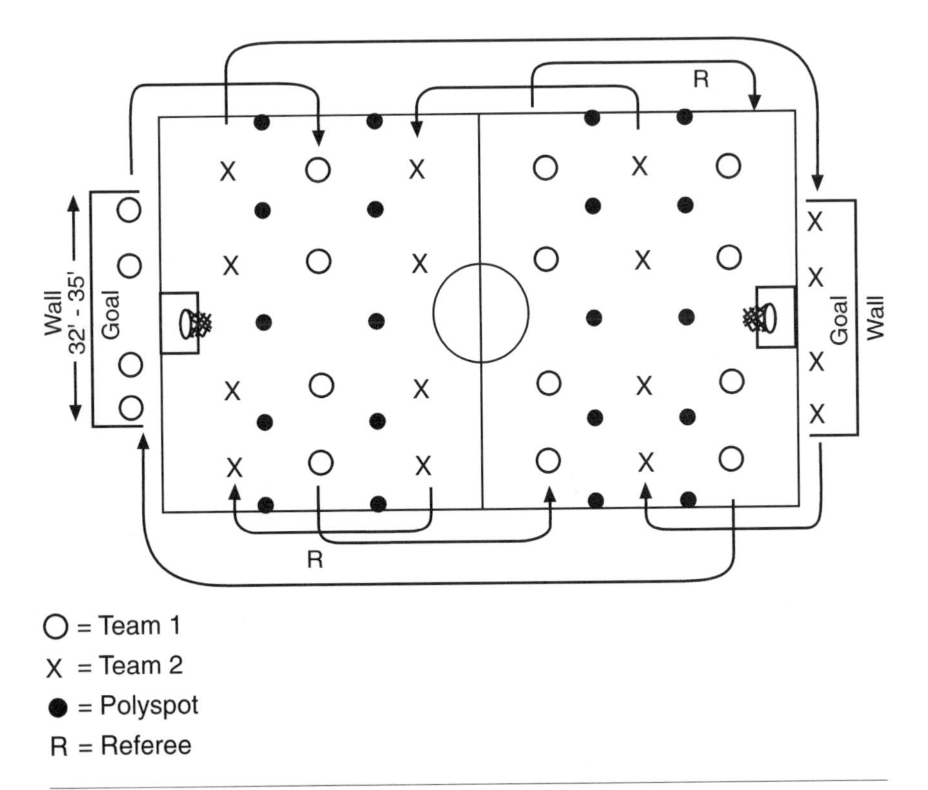

Figure 10.6 Rotational pattern for Foosball Kaleidoscope.

- Basketball Goals: All shots that are made are worth four points. Upon a successful shot through the hoop, the ball is given to an opposing team's goalie who will immediately put the ball in play. When this ball is given to a goalie, no points are awarded if it hits the wall. Note, time is not called when a score occurs, and goalies should play the ball out as quickly as possible so they can be ready for a scoring attempt using another ball.

Safety Considerations

The chance of injury is very small since foam balls are being used. A goalie who attempts to stop with his hands a ball kicked by one of the outermost court players is at greatest risk. Since balls must hit within the taped area for a kicked ball to count, encourage goalies to use their feet when they are playing close to the endline.

Helpful Hints

Prior to adding a third ball, be sure that players are familiar with the rules. After each player rotation, remind the lines of the requirements each must follow when playing the ball.

Volley-Foosball Variation

A court and player setup similar to those described in the Kaleidoscope version are used; however, two or three foam volleyballs that will bounce to some degree should be substituted, and court players may not use their feet to play the ball. Only volleyball skills are used by everyone except the goalies, who may use any part of their bodies to protect the goal. If a shot at the basket is attempted by the line of players closest to the opposing goal, then the individual executing that shot may catch the ball prior to trying to score in the hoop. On all other shots, the ball must be sent into the goal on the wall from another player's direct hit or pass. If the ball falls to the ground, players must use volleyball skills to send the ball into the air unless the ball is rolling on the floor. In that instance, a player is permitted to pick up the ball and volley it to another player. No double hits are permitted. If a player catches a ball and then passes it or if the ball is rolling and a player picks it up and passes it, only a single hit has occurred. Should a double hit occur, the ball is given to the line of opponents that is nearest to the goal in which they are attempting to score. Depending on the skill level of the players, the instructor may want to allow all players to catch the ball prior to completing a pass. Because basketball goals will be more difficult to score, increase their point value to four or five. Each ball sent to the wall goal from the catch would be worth one point, while those played directly from a pass earn two points.

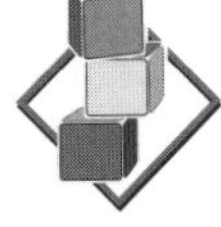

Adaptations for Younger Participants

This activity is suitable for grades four and five if the following rule changes are applied. Do not permit the outermost two lines of court players to use their hands for any play whatsoever, including blocking of goalie passes and playing the ball when they receive the ball because of a violation by the goalies during a non-scoring situation. Since shots at the basket must be taken from lines of players located nearest the centerline, the chance of scoring is small. To improve the odds, award one point for any ball that hits the basketball rim. Give younger participants adequate practice to become accustomed to not being able to pick up the ball directly from the floor, and teach them the techniques for a self-tip-up and for lofting the ball to another player.

BASKET-MAZEBALL

Basket-Mazeball combines a dribbling relay with basketball skills and dodgeball skills, using a nontraditional player configuration for a large group of participants. Pairs of players working together must weave through a maze of stationary opponents while dribbling a basketball and passing to a designated area where they have one shot to try to make a basket without being hit by a ball at or below waist level.

Objectives

Develops dribbling, passing, throwing, and shooting skills; enhances agility and speed.

Equipment

Three to four basketballs, two foam soccer balls, four cones to define the boundaries, an additional four to six cones to specify where the first person from each line will be positioned when they are on the offensive, and one polyspot for each of the defensive players.

Playing Area

A basketball court will permit 20 to 30 per team. With fewer individuals, reduce the length of the court by approximately one-quarter, and if necessary, decrease the width by up to 10 feet (3.0 meters). The size of the playing area should allow approximately 10 to 11 feet (3.0 to 3.4 meters) between each defensive player. This will give the dribbler about 3 to 4 feet (0.9 to 1.2 meters) to maneuver between pairs of defensive players, who must maintain at least one foot on their marking spot at all times unless they are retrieving a foam ball from out-of-bounds.

Participants

Twenty to 30 per team. Two to three officials.

Game

Form two equal teams with the offensive team members in an even number of lines consisting of three or four players each and positioned behind one of the cones on an endline. It is immaterial if adjacent lines have an equal number of participants. The defense spreads out over the court, leaving about 10 to 11 feet (3.0 to 3.4 meters) between one another. A marking spot should be placed on the court to designate a given defender's position. With larger numbers of participants, the defense should arrange themselves in staggered rows to cover the entire playing area. Figure 10.7 shows a court design for 30 players per team.

To begin the game, the first person in each of the even numbered lines is holding a basketball, and two of the individuals in the odd numbered lines are holding a foam soccer ball. At the whistle, the players holding the foam balls will put them into play by kicking or throwing them forward so that each bounces at least once within the playing area or touches

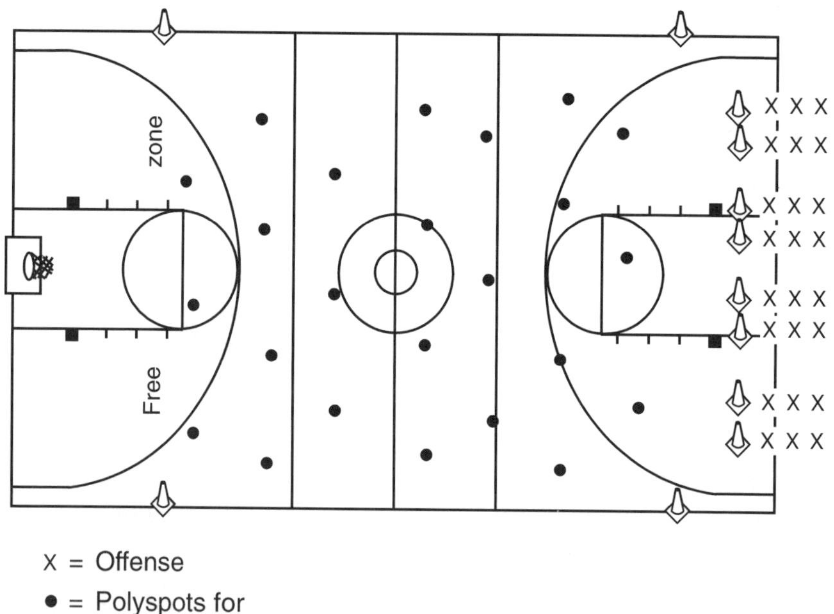

Figure 10.7 Basket-Mazeball court design and player setup.

a defensive player. This initial action is just a means of beginning play and is not an important offensive weapon. The same is true for the start of each half inning, because the defense must complete two passes with each ball before that foam ball can be used to hit offensive players. These requirements give the first persons in pairs of lines who will be working together a few seconds to decide the path they will take to avoid being hit and avoid having the basketball stolen or knocked away by a defensive player whose team then gains possession.

The first participants in lines 1 and 2, 3 and 4, and so on, work together to dribble and pass the basketball down the court so that the individual who has control of the basketball is not hit with a foam ball at waist level or below and does not have the basketball stolen or knocked away and secured by one of the defenders. Additionally, these players may not double-dribble or travel. The defenders must keep at least one foot on their marking spot but are permitted to switch their pivot foot. If the pair is successful in weaving through the maze of players and gets to the free zone, one shot is taken at the basket on the far end of the court, with the shooter standing outside of the lane. It is illogical for the defense to throw at individuals when they are in this safety area, as it would not result in earning an out.

Two points are scored if both players from a pair successfully make it down the court through the maze. If the basket is good, it is awarded two or three points, depending upon whether or not the shot is made from behind the three-point arc. After the shot is taken, the players again attempt to negotiate through the maze, trying to earn another two points by bringing the ball back to the next individual in either of the two lines from which the pair started.

Each offensive pair may choose any path within the playing area to elude the defense. They may change directions, go sideways, use a defensive player as a shield, and so on. Care must be taken to avoid coming too close to a defender who can steal the ball. Once a person in the pair with control of the ball is hit at or below waist level, both players in the pair should exit out the side of the court as quickly as possible, returning the basketball to the next individual in either of their two lines. They then join the back of the line in which they were originally positioned to wait for the opportunity to attempt to score again. Thus, being hit at the waist or below does not eliminate either player from the game.

Play is continuous until a total of six offensive mistakes (outs) occur coming from either a loss of control of the basketball so that a defensive player gains possession of the ball, a player is hit at or below waist level while he has the ball in his possession, or a player double-dribbles or travels. Each time a mistake occurs, the official who observed the play should call out loudly the number of outs for the defensive team. All referees should keep track of the number of outs by holding up the appropriate number of fingers to let the defense know how many more offensive mistakes must occur before the half inning is over. Each referee should attempt to watch one or two pairs on offense. The official who calls the sixth out blows a whistle to stop the action. Before players exchange positions, the players on the odd number offensive lines indicate the number of points their pair earned within that half inning. To be sure that each pair of players has an equal opportunity to earn points, have the last pair on offense from the previous inning go to the end of the line when the team returns to the offense, and require that if player A in the pair took the last shot at the basket, then player B in the pair must take the next shot. A game usually consists of five to eight innings, with the team earning the greatest number of points declared the winner.

Additional Rules

A defensive player must have at least one foot on her marking spot, except to chase a foam ball that has rolled outside the playing area. When a ball rolls out-of-bounds, the closest player retrieves it. That player must run back to his position and complete two passes within the defense before the ball may be used to hit an offensive player. The same two-pass requirement applies to the beginning of each half inning.

A fly caught from the opening kick or throw is played like any other ball. This game is not like bombardment, in which the player would be considered out.

A pair is out if within the defensive court boundaries

- a player who has possession of the ball is hit at or below the waist.
- the defense steals or bats the ball away and a defender is able to gain possession before one of the players from that twosome can do so (Note, it is legal for a player who is about to be hit to use the basketball as a shield, have her partner serve as the shield, place the ball on the floor for no more than 10 seconds, pass the ball to herself or her partner, and so on.).
- a player double-dribbles.
- an offensive player steps out-of-bounds beyond the sidelines of the area that the defense is protecting.
- the player travels while dribbling. In the safety zone, double-dribbling and traveling are not called.

If an offensive player places the ball down on the court for more than 10 seconds, the pair is out.

When an out occurs, the pair must exit the nearest side of the court. If a defender has gained possession of the basketball, the ball is rolled to that side of the court. The pair should return to their lines and rejoin at the back after giving the basketball to one of the players at the front of either of their lines.

Players may remain in the free zone for 25 seconds before they must leave. If either player in a pair reenters the safety zone before scoring additional points or being hit at or below the waist, the pair is out. If possible, an official should give a five-second warning.

If a player is hit with the ball while in the free zone, the pair is not out and play continues.

If a defender violates one of the rules in the process of stealing a basketball or picking up a loose basketball, or she fouls a member of the offensive team, the offensive pair is not out and is awarded a free one-way trip, along with the points that normally accompany the movement to or from the safety zone.

Each pair of players represents a unit that must work together. Changing partners is not permitted within a half inning and results in an out.

If an offensive player purposely pushes, shoves, or throws the basketball at a defensive player in a dangerous way to avoid being hit or losing his dribble, or to gain an advantage for the offense, the pair is automatically out.

A shot that is taken from within the lane earns no points regardless of whether or not the basket was made.

A player who has control of the ball while dribbling is deemed to be in possession of the ball.

Safety Considerations

Make sure participants understand that the defense should aim at the legs of the players who have control of the ball and not above their waists.

Helpful Hints

Remind pairs they must keep track of their own points with two points earned for each successful one-way trip through the maze and two or three points depending upon where the basket is made from a one-shot attempt. Offensive strategy suggests that once an individual is in danger of a defender knocking the ball away, the person should pick up his dribble and look to complete a short pass to his partner. To ward off foam ball shots aimed at the players controlling the basketballs, if one's partner is not in position to receive a pass, it is often advantageous to turn and face the thrower and use the basketball to divert the foam ball, as a person's body must be hit at or below waist level in order for an out to occur. To avoid being hit while one has possession of the basketball, a self-toss may be employed, the ball may be momentarily placed on the court out of reach of the defense, or the other person in the pair who does not have control of the ball may serve as a shield. If any of these tactics is employed, the defense can offset this strategy by faking a throw before actually attempting to hit the player. Because of the number of balls used in this game, there is a great deal of action, and officiating is not especially easy. It is inevitable that some outs will be missed, unless players are encouraged and willing to monitor themselves closely.

Volley-Mazeball Variation

Two volleyballs will be used in place of the basketballs. Because volleyball actions are not as accurate and controlled as basketball dribbling and passing, different rules will have to be integrated, along with modification in the player setup. The number of individuals that make up the maze should be reduced by one-third to one-half. Equally space out five cones along the width of the court behind which three or four players from the offensive team will be positioned. Rather than having pairs of players work together, the first person in each line represents one volleying group, the second person in line the second volleying group, and so on. The object of this team is to pass the ball among their group using volleyball skills, such that the ball is sent into the free zone after a minimum of five passes, where each member of the group has completed at least one pass and where the ball must rise at least six feet (1.8 meters) high on each pass. The Mazeball team attempts to use the foam soccer-sized balls to contact the volleyball while it is airborne. If this occurs before the team reaches the safety area in five or more passes, then an out occurs. Three outs, and the maze team will change with the volleying team. Points are earned for each successful pass the team completes. The volleying team is allowed to catch the volleyball a total of three times while trying to traverse the maze. Once a ball is caught, the player is allowed to take one step before executing a pass within five seconds. If either the five-second or one-step rule is violated, then that pass does not count in the total. Should more than three catches be used by a team, then on the fourth catch, an automatic out is awarded. If the ball hits the floor, it counts as a catch, but no pass is awarded on that action. If the ball is sent into the free zone and less than five passes have been completed, no points are awarded and an out is recorded. As in volleyball, no double hits are permitted for the team attempting to pass the volleyball down court. Once an out has occurred or a team has successfully gotten the volleyball to the safety zone, the next volleying group begins to traverse the maze, and the first fivesome return to their respective lines giving their volleyball to the third wave of players. The same basic regulations apply to the maze team unless specified above. During play, it is helpful if one of the referees keeps track of catches for each group as they work through the maze and number of outs.

References and Suggested Sources

Adams, J.L. 1986. *The care and feeding of ideas: A guide to encouraging creativity.* Reading, MA: Addison-Wesley.

Bok, D. 1986. *Higher learning.* Cambridge, MA: Harvard University Press.

Bratt, S. 1982. "A process for teaching inventive games." *Florida Journal of Health, Physical Education and Recreation* 2:3–20.

Dietz, W.H., and Gortmaker, S.L. 1985. "Do we fatten our children at the television set? Obesity and television viewing in children and adolescents." *Pediatrics* 75:807–812.

Fluegelman, A., ed. 1976. *The new games book.* Garden City, NY: Dolphin Books/Doubleday.

Haefele, J.W. 1962. *Creativity and innovation.* New York: Reinhold.

Holt, J. 1974. *Escape from childhood.* New York: Holt Associates.

Lichtman, B. 1993. *Innovative games.* Champaign, IL: Human Kinetics.

Mooney, R., and Razik, T. 1967. *Explorations in creativity.* New York: Harper & Row.

Nieman, D.C. 1990. *Fitness and sports medicine: An introduction.* Palo Alto, CA: Bull.

Ochse, R. 1990. *Before the gates of excellence.* Cambridge, MA: Cambridge University Press.

Orlick, T. 1978. *The cooperative sports & games book.* New York: Pantheon Books.

Parnes, S.J., and Harding, H.F. 1962. *A source book for creative thinking.* New York: Scribner and Sons.

Porte, J. 1983. *Emerson essays and lectures.* New York: Literary Classics of America.

Reber, A.S. 1985. *The Penguin dictionary of psychology.* Harmondsworth, Middlesex: Penguin.

Sarason, S.B. 1990. *The predictable failure of educational reform.* San Francisco: Jossey-Bass.

Schlechty, P.C. 1990. *Schools for the 21st century.* San Francisco: Jossey-Bass.

Shank, R. 1988. *The creative attitude: Learning to ask and answer the right questions.* New York: Macmillan.

Silberman, C.E. 1970. *Crisis in the classroom: The remaking of American education.* New York: Random House.

Smith, C.F. 1935. *Games and game leadership.* New York: Dodd, Mead.

Steinberg, R.J., ed. 1988. *The nature of creativity.* Cambridge, MA: Cambridge University Press.

Toch, T. 1991. *In the name of excellence.* New York: Oxford University Press.

Tye, K.A., and Novotney, J.M. 1975. *Schools in transition: The practitioner as change agent.* New York: McGraw-Hill.

White, J.R., ed. 1990. *Sports rules encyclopedia.* Champaign, IL: Human Kinetics.

Index

Note: Page numbers in *italic* indicate illustrations; those in **boldface** indicate tables.

A

Action Clue 136-141
- twelve-station court setup 136, *138*
- twelve-station setup 136, **137**

activities. *See also* games
- altered 65-81
- hybrid 25-44
- multi-principled 161-180

Adams, J.L. 2, 181

adaptations
- multimedia 123-145
- for younger participants. *See specific games*

additive approach 10-11

altered actions 65-81

"American Gladiators" 8, 141

attitude
- "if it's not broken, don't fix it" 11
- what-if 5

B

badminton-type games
- Hand-Minton 119-122, *120*
- Milk Jug-Minton 119-122, *121*
- Tic-Tac-Toe, Badminton version 125, 127-128

baseball games. *See also* softball games
- Box Baseball 89-93, *91*
- Dot Baseball 89-93, *90*
- Punchball in the Round 97-100
- Running Bases 84-86, *86*

basketball games
- Basket Hoop Bombardment 87-88, **88,** *89*
- Basket-Mazeball **162,** 175-180, *176*
- Dodge Basketball 31-34, *32, 33*
- Flag Basketball 26, 35-37, *36*
- Roller Trash Can Basketball **135,** 141-145, *142, 143*
- Tennis Backboard Basketball 95-97, *96*
- Three-Armed Basketball 79-81, *80*

Basket Hoop Bombardment 87-88
- modified court design for younger participants 88, *89*
- scoring options **88**

Basket-Mazeball **162,** 175-180
- court design and player setup 176, *176*
- Volley-Mazeball variation **162,** 180

Battleship 124, 129-132
- court setup and player configuration 130, *130*

Beachball Locomotion 74-77
- derriere-to-derriere transport 75, *76*
- different body part transport 76-77
- forehead-to-forehead transport 75, *75*
- same body part transport *75,* 75-76, *76*

board games 124-125

Bok, D. 2-3, 181

Bombardment Derby (case history) 18-23, *21*
- court setup for 20-22, *22*
- subsequent changes 23

bombardment games
- Basket Hoop Bombardment 87-88
- Bombardment Derby (case history) 18-23, *21, 22*
- Cone Slide Bombardment 111-113, *112*
- Limb Bombardment 77-79, *78*
- Towel Ball Pin Bombardment 58-61, *60*

Bottlecap Golf 47-50
- sample hole *49*

bowling games
- Battleship 124, 129-132, *130*
- Frisbee Skeet Bowling 116-119, *117, 118*
- Rebound Bowling 148-151, *150, 151*
- Towel Ball Pin Bombardment 58-61, *60*

Box Baseball 89-93
  court design and player setup 91, *91*
brainstorming
  small-group 9-10
  “think tank” stations 7
broadening experiences 7-8
  steps for 8

C

case history 18-22, *21, 22*
  initial meeting 18-19
  second meeting 19-21
  subsequent changes 23
  third meeting 21-22
“coloring book” approach 4
Cone Slide Bombardment 111-113
  court design and player setup 111, *112*
Corner Ball 159-160
  court layout 159, *160*
creativity 3-4
  encouraging 1-11
  guidelines for encouraging 4, *4*
  professional’s role in 4-7
  starting point 7-10
  unlocking 2-3
croquet games. *See* Soccer Croquet–Four Ways

D

developing hybrid activities 25-44
  schema for 25-26, **26**
Dietz, W.H. 8, 181
divergent thinking 5
Dodge Basketball 31-34, *33*
  player positioning 32, *32*
Dot Baseball 89-93
  court layout *90,* 90-91

E

effective elements 7
encouraging creativity 1-11
  guidelines for 4, *4*
Endline Ball 113-116, *114*
  court design and player setup 113-114, *114*
equipment. *See also specific games*
  expense criterion for 16
  multimedia adaptations 123-145
  new uses for 107-122
  nontraditional 45-64
expense criterion 16

F

field days, intramural 11
Flag Basketball 26, 35-37
  start of a play 35, *36*
foosball games
  Foosball Kaleidoscope **162,** 171-175, *172, 173*
  Pole Foosball 132-135, *133, 134,* **162**
  Volley-Foosball **162,** 174
Foosball Kaleidoscope **162,** 171-175
  court and player setup 171, *172*
  rotational pattern 173, *173*
  Volley-Foosball variation 174
football games
  Milk Jug Football 61-64
  Soccer Flag Football 26, 38-40, *39,* **39**
Frisbee Skeet Bowling 116-119, *118*
  court design and player setup 116-117, *117*
Frisbee Soccer 108-111, *110*
  court design and player setup 108-109, *109*
Frontline Shift Volleyball 102-105
  modified shifting pattern for less skilled players 105, *106*
  shifting patterns 102-103, *103, 104*

G

game creation
  additive approach to 10-11
  case history 18-23, *21, 22*
  effective elements for 7
  factors to consider during 5, **6**
  hints for 15-16
  most often asked questions 14-17
  multi-principled creations 161-180
  nurturing process 18-19
games 13-23. *See also specific games*
  altered 65-81
  board games 124-125
  common elements of 5
  effective elements of 7
  hybrid 26-44
  innovative 2-3, 15, 16-17
  with modified goals and player setup 84-106
  multimedia adaptations 125-145
  multi-principled 163-180
  names of 17-18
  with new uses for standard equipment 108-122
  with nontraditional equipment 46-64
  pinball games 124
  questions for 84
  similar 14-15
  with unique locales and underused spaces 148-160
  video games 124
  work in progress 13-23
games book 9
goals, modifying 83-106
golf games. *See* Bottlecap Golf
Gortmaker, S.L. 8, 181

H
Haefele, J.W. 2, 3, 181
Hallball Three Ways 152-156, *154, 155*
  court design for narrow hallways 152, *153*
Hand-Minton 119-122, *120*
Harding, H.F. 2, 181
hints 15-16
Holt, J. 2, 181
hybrid activities
  developing 25-44
  games 26-44
  schema for developing 25-26, **26**

I
ideas, manipulation of 5
"if it's not broken, don't fix it" attitude 11
incubation time 6-7
innovative games 15, 16-17
  discovering 2-3
  evolution of 13-23
  most often asked questions about 14-17
  nurturing process for 18-22
  questions for 84
intramural, field-day experiences 11

J
"Jeopardy" 8

L
let's-try-it approach 5
Lichtman, B. ix, *4,* 18, 124, 147, 162, **162,** 181
Limb Bombardment 77-79, *78*
locales, unique 147-160

M
manipulation of ideas and objects 5
Mazeball **162**
  Basket-Mazeball **162,** 175-180, *176*
  Volley-Mazeball **162,** 180
Milk Jug Football 61-64
  field setup 62, *62*
  start of play 63, *63*
Milk Jug-Minton 119-122, *121*
Mooney, R. 2, 181
multimedia adaptations 123-145
Multi-Option Ball 26, 40-44
  court design 41, *41*
  scoring possibilities **42**
multi-principled creations 161-180
  schema for developing 161-162, **162**

N
Naismith 7
names of games 17-18
Novotney, J.M. 3, 182
nurturing process, case history 18-22

O
objects, manipulation of 5
obstacle courses 16
  Basket-Mazeball **162,** 175-180, *176*
  Volley-Mazeball **162,** 180
Ochse, R. 2, 181
"oh, that again" syndrome 2, 11
Olympics 4
Olympic extravaganza 11
One-Walled Volleyball 156-159
  court setup 156, *157*

P
Parnes, S.J. 2, 181
pinball games 124
player setup. *See also specific games*
  modifying 83-106
Pole Foosball 132-135, *134,* **162**
  court design, player setup, and ball positioning 132, *133*
  rotational sequence 134, **135**
Porte, J. 2, 181
professionals 4-7
Punchball in the Round 97-100
  field design and player setup 98, *98*

R
Razik, T. 2, 181
Reber, A.S. 3, 181
Rebound Bowling 148-151, *150, 151*
  possibilities 149
  score sheet and trajectory requirements 149, *150*
recreational board games 124-125
relays or obstacle courses 16
  Basket-Mazeball **162,** 175-180, *176*
  Volley-Mazeball **162,** 180
Ricochet Fungo Softball 163-167, *166*
  field design and player setup 163, *164*
  player setup and court design 163, *164*
Roller Trash Can Basketball 141-145, *143*
  court setup 142, *142*
  rotational sequence **135**
Running Bases 84-86, *86*
  version one 85
  version two 86

S
sanctions 5-6
Sarason, S.B. 2, 181
Schlechty, P.C. 2, 182
Scooterized Volleyball *72,* 72-74
Scooter Slalom 66-72
  back-to-back runs 69, *69*
  courses 67, *68*

Scooter Slalom *(continued)*
  individual plunger runs 69, *70*
  locomotor possibilities *69,* 69-71, *70*
sensitivity to common elements 5
Shank, R. 2, 3, 182
Sheetball Brigade 54-58
  field and player setup 54, *55*
  passing and catching actions 56, *56*
Silberman, C.E. 2, 182
small-group brainstorming 9-10
Soccer Croquet–Four Ways 26-31, *28*
  version one 28
  version two 29
  version three 29
  version four *29,* 29-30
Soccer Flag Football 26, 38-40, *39*
  player position involvement 38, **39**
soccer games
  Frisbee Soccer 108-111, *109, 110*
  Soccer Croquet–Four Ways 26-31, *28, 29*
  Soccer Flag Football 26, 38-40, *39,* **39**
  Soft-Volley-Soccer *168,* 168-171
softball games. *See also* baseball games
  Punchball in the Round 97-100
  Ricochet Fungo Softball 163-167, *164, 166*
  Soft-Volley-Soccer *168,* 168-171
  Tic-Tac-Toe; Pitch, Hit, and Rebound version 125, 127
  Tic-Tac-Toe, Pitch and Hit version 125, 127
Soft Goalball 18
Soft-Volleyball 93-95
  court design and player setup 93, *94*
Soft-Volley-Soccer 168-171
  field configuration and player setup 168, *168*
spaces, underused 147-160
starting point 7-10
Steinberg, R.J. 2, 3, 182
students
  most often asked questions by 14-17
  work in progress 13-23

T

Team Tennis-Volley 100-102
television 123-124
Tennis Backboard Basketball 95-97
  court design for 95, *96*
tennis games
  Team Tennis-Volley 100-102
  Tennis Backboard Basketball 95-97, *96*
  Volley-Tennis Broom Ball 50-54, *51, 52, 53*
terminology 3-4
thinking
  "coloring book" approach to 4
  divergent 5
"think tank" stations 7
Three-Armed Basketball 79-81, *80*
Tic-Tac-Toe Multiple Ways 125-128
  additional variations **128-129**
  Badminton version 125, 127-128
  general court design and player positioning 125-126, *126*
  Pitch, Hit, and Rebound version 125, 127
  Pitch and Hit version 125, 127
Toch, T. 2, 182
tolerance 5-6
Towel Ball Pin Bombardment 58-61, *60*
toys 16
Treasure Hunt 124
Tye, K.A. 3, 182

U

underused spaces 147-160

V

video games 124
videos 8-9
violations. *See specific games*
volleyball games
  Frontline Shift Volleyball 102-105, *103, 104, 106*
  One-Walled Volleyball 156-159
  Scooterized Volleyball *72,* 72-74
  Soft-Volleyball 93-95, *94*
  Soft-Volley-Soccer *168,* 168-171
  Team Tennis-Volley 100-102
  Volley-Foosball **162,** 174
  Volley-Mazeball **162,** 180
  Volley-Tennis Broom Ball 50-54, *51, 52, 53*
Volley-Foosball **162,** 174
Volley-Mazeball **162,** 180
Volley-Tennis Broom Ball 50-54, *53*
  tennis court layout 50, *52*
  volleyball court design 50, *51*

W

what-if attitude 5
"Wheel of Fortune" 8
Wright, Terry 18

About the Author

Brenda Lichtman is a professor of kinesiology at Sam Houston State University in Huntsville, Texas. Tired of hearing "Oh, that again" from students and teachers alike, Brenda has worked since 1972 on infusing physical education curricula with new life through the use of innovative games. She has presented her ideas at more than 45 local, national, and international forums and written several scholarly articles on the subject. The importance of this work has resulted in an innovative games class becoming part of the kinesiology curriculum at Sam Houston State.

Brenda received a PhD in physical education from the University of Maryland at College Park in 1976. She has served as editor-in-chief of the *Journal of Educational Studies* and has been a member of the editorial review board of the *Texas Journal of Physical Education, Health, Recreation and Dance*; the *Journal of Physical Education, Recreation and Dance*; and *Strategies*. During her career, Brenda has twice been a finalist for the excellence in teaching award given by Sam Houston State University. She is a member of the Texas Alliance of Health, Physical Education, Recreation and Dance and the American Alliance of Health, Physical Education, Recreation and Dance. In her free time, Brenda enjoys cycling, backpacking, canoeing, and playing pickleball.

Related Books From Human Kinetics

Innovative Games

Brenda Lichtman

1993 • Paperback • 144 pp • Item BLIC0488
ISBN 0-87322-488-4 • $16.00 ($23.95 Canadian)
35 ready-to-use activities for students in grades 6 through 12.

Changing Kids' Games

Second Edition

Don Morris and Jim Stiehl

1999 • Paperback • 148 pp • Item BMOR0691
ISBN 0-88011-691-9 • $17.00 ($25.50 Canadian)
Second edition shows teachers how to modify games to suit all children's developmental needs. Helps teachers select, plan, modify, present, and evaluate movement games to fit their purposes, values, styles, and resources. For children in grades K-8.

Multicultural Games

Lorraine Barbarash

1997 • Paperback • 152 pp • Item BBAR0565
ISBN 0-88011-565-3 • $14.95 ($21.95 Canadian)
Features 75 games from 43 countries or cultures on 6 continents, this practical reference is an excellent source for building an interdisciplinary and multicultural curriculum. Can also help educators meet NASPE's national content standards for multicultural awareness at the elementary and middle school level.

Cooperative Learning in Physical Education

Steven Grineski

1996 • Paperback • 152 pp • Item BGRI0879
ISBN 0-87322-879-0 • $16.00 ($23.95 Canadian)
Helps educators teach students to value each other through positive interdependence, individual accountability, and collaborative skills. Explains how to develop cooperative learning lessons.

To request more information or to order, U.S. customers call 1-800-747-4457, e-mail us at humank@hkusa.com, or visit our Web site at http://www.humankinetics.com/. Persons outside the U.S. can contact us via our Web site or use the appropriate telephone number, postal address, or e-mail address shown in the front of this book.

HUMAN KINETICS
The Information Leader in Physical Activity
P.O. Box 5076, Champaign, IL 61825-5076
2335